SCOTT HOUSTON

MOMENTUM

HOW TO **REGAIN** AND **MAINTAIN** YOUR **EDGE**

ISBN: 978-1-943361-16-8
E-Book ISBN: 978-1-943361-17-5

Library of Congress Control Number: 2016951271

Printed in the United States of America.

Contents

Preface

As I was praying about the development of this book, I began to think about the Bible studies for men in which I have been a participant through the years, and the "how to" instructional books for men that I've read. Many of those were very good, and my concern was that men would look at this book and without opening it, place it in the "done that" category and miss the encouragement and energy that God has infused into these pages. The message of this material is that *we men*, the priests of our homes, and the leaders in our communities, *may be equipped to live extraordinary lives.* We should also be the catalyst for change in our churches. Not doctrinal change...not change in the template that God has inspired our church leaders to implement for our services and training. But we *can* cause a shift in the balance of POWER involved in our everyday effort to bring captivity captive and to really do the greater works that we know we should be doing. We should also be leaders and examples at our workplaces.

I continually meet with Christian men who have become frustrated with their lives; who are wishing and hoping for victory over situations and circumstances that have become major hindrances in their efforts to take new ground. Many have lost their passion for their marriages, jobs, maybe for life itself. These are good men, hard workers, doing all that they know to do for their families, careers and relationships. Yet if you asked them point-blank, *"Are you feeling fulfilled?"* most (if not all) would say no. Just think what would happen to our churches, businesses, nation and world if Christian men experienced dramatically new excitement, power and authority. You know…the kind that is promised us in the Bible! What if men really laid hands on the sick and they recovered. Think people would notice? What if men today truly walked in wisdom concerning their marriages and families. Think our wives would notice? What if we were the most honest, dedicated, supportive employees in the workplace. Would our bosses notice? What if we really were the lenders and not the borrowers, prospering in every good work. Think people would notice? I find that virtually all men want great things for themselves and their families.

That is why this book is an important resource. We have to become the men whose wives and children respect and honor. We should become the employees that fellow workers want to work with and that employers can depend on. We can be the business leaders that others trust. And we are certainly needed as the faithful volunteers that form the backbone of every thriving church.

The chapters in this book are all directed toward men. But they apply to men, women and children. So, guys please take the information from this book and teach it to your families. I know you will be blessed as you read and reread this book.

Acknowledgements

Special thanks to:

James R. Bruce, deceased, former pastor of Hope Church, St. Louis, Missouri. The foundation of my Christian life was established at his church. I am grateful to him and to his family for caring for us when we were young newlyweds searching for real purpose in our lives.

My current pastor and friend, Pastor Bill Scheer of Guts Church in Tulsa, Skiatook and Sapulpa, Oklahoma, has sown so much into my life. I couldn't begin to share all that he has done for me. But one very important thing he has taught me is that Christian men (probably all men) aren't truly fulfilled until they step outside of their comfort zones and focus on helping others. With him I continually find myself in uncomfortable situations. But this always causes me to grow and I am very thankful.

Hunter, my son, and Shaun and Harold, my sons-in-law, exemplify what Christian men can be. Even though they are young men, they are already incredible leaders. I aspire to be like them.

I know this is primarily a men's book, but I have to acknowledge the most important person in my life, Vanessa. One of

her many amazing gifts is her ability to encourage me to not settle for "good enough" even when I normally would. "Good enough" doesn't bring momentum. Somehow she draws out the very best in everyone.

Chapter One

Change What?

If you have looked at the titles of some of the other chapters, you might feel that several of the others would be more appropriate to begin our study. I wrestled with that as I wrote this chapter, and I had even considered placing it last. Why? Because we must be willing to let the principles in the other chapters facilitate the adjustments that we need to make in and about ourselves. If we are obedient and sincere, we will become the successful, *fulfilled* men that God intends us to be. I purposely opened the book with this chapter because, though many men feel they need to change things in their lives, they believe they really CAN'T change them. Honestly, some men haven't really put up a worthy fight. Others have tried to change, but found that they simply went back to their old behaviors. Some are waiting for the Holy Spirit to simply take over their will and cause the needed changes to manifest! It is essential for men to know that though change is sometimes difficult, *it is absolutely possible*. If you will accept that premise, then the principles in the following chapters will benefit you greatly.

I had the opportunity to pray with Joe during the altar call near the end of a Sunday evening service at our church. He had been going through what he termed a "living Hell." He was recently divorced, hated his job, and was extremely lonely. He came to the realization that he needed a change in his life and believed that responding to the altar call was going to be the beginning of a better kind of life. He told me that he had given his life to the Lord years ago, but that he had never really grown close to God and that other things had become more important to him. He was tearful as he explained how much he hated his life. As I led him in a prayer of repentance, when he told God he was sorry for not putting Him first, he was so choked up that he could hardly utter the words. A real healing took place and he left church with new purpose.

Months later, Joe was back at the altar, needing prayer. He told me that he felt like he had made a commitment to God and was going to experience a new life when we prayed the last time. But he didn't change any of the behaviors that wrecked his life the first time. The things that came between him and God before came between them again. So here he was…back where he had started. He was frustrated and helpless.

We all have the ability to identify aspects of our lives that could use some adjustment. These may be attitudes. They may be behaviors. They may be techniques. They may be our relationships. The problem is that though it is easy to recognize the need to change, it is much more difficult to actually make the change! Don't believe me? Here's a simple exercise. Cross your arms in front of you. You know how. You do it every time you want to put off someone who is trying to sell you some-

thing. Now, reverse your arms. I'll be patient! It will take a minute or two for some of you. Or try this one. Fold your hands like you're going to pray. Now reverse them. It feels awkward, doesn't it? It's almost like they don't fit at all. Finally, write your name using the opposite hand you normally use. You can do it, but it takes a lot of concentration and effort.

We become so accustomed to doing things a certain way that it seems impossible to change them. But we also can become accustomed to even thinking a certain way or acting a certain way. We are told that our personalities and mannerisms are fully developed in our early years. I have three grown children, and I can attest to the fact that their personalities have been consistent from around the time that they first began to walk. Each is unique. And each required a different approach in dealing with life's issues. It sure would have been helpful to have a manual that explained exactly how to handle each one in every situation!

Men are the victims of the mores of society more than anyone else. Men receive instructions from many different places on how they should think and act. Their upbringing certainly has a major influence on their attitudes and behaviors. Their schools, workplaces and churches are influential. Today, however, men (and especially boys) are receiving incredibly persuasive input from television and the internet. The pressure to conform is immense. To "fight the system" seems like a daunting task. Taking a stand for minimum standards often requires a fight of faith. Take a simple thing like movies. How many of us have sat through a movie when the entire time we had an incredibly uneasy feeling inside? How often have we felt

bad when we left the theater? We agreed to go in the first place because we would have felt weird by simply not going with all of our friends. I'm not making any kind of judgment on movies or going to them, but it's a simple example of how society influences us. Television is an incredibly persuasive mechanism. We are bombarded with shows and advertisements that tell us what to wear, what to eat and drink and what type of lifestyle is acceptable and popular. Many shows are so subtle that we find ourselves accepting things that we would normally never accept. I'm amazed at what men are willing to compromise when the message is softened enough to seem palatable.

The simple fact is that *we can change*. Men do not have to live a life that frustrates and angers them. Sometimes change comes very easily and sometimes it takes a while. The Apostle John is a great Biblical example of someone who changed. He has been called the "disciple of love" through the years. In fact, 1 John has often been used for teaching how God expects us to treat others.

1 John 4:7,8: "Beloved, let us love one another, for love is of God; and everyone who loves is born of God and knows God. He who does not love does not know God, for God is love."

1 John 4:16: "And we have known and believed the love that God has for us. God is love, and he who abides in love abides in God, and God in him."

1 John 4:18: "There is no fear in love; but perfect love casts out fear, because fear involves torment. But he who fears has not been made perfect in love."

1 John 4:21: "And this commandment we have from Him: that he who loves God must love his brother also."

From these scriptures you would think that John was always living exactly what these verses express. But that isn't so. In Mark 3:17 Jesus called John and his brother James Boanerges, or Sons of Thunder. Why? James and John could be uppity, condescending and judgmental. Their attitudes might have been a result of their upbringing. Their father, Zebedee, was well-known. Their home may have been one of affluence. For whatever reason, James and John were anything but examples of the love walk that John instructs in his epistles. And Jesus had to correct their attitude toward others, even to the point of rebuking them. Here are three examples.

Luke 9:49,50: Now John answered and said, "Master, we saw someone casting out demons in Your name, and we forbade him because he does not follow with us." But Jesus said to him, "Do not forbid him, for he who is not against us is on our side."

Luke 9:51-56: Now it came to pass, when the time had come for Him to be received up, that He steadfastly set His face to go to Jerusalem, and sent messengers before His face. And as they went, they entered a village of the Samaritans, to prepare for Him. But they did not receive Him, because His face was set for the journey to Jerusalem. And when His disciples James and John saw this, they said, "Lord, do You want us to command fire to come down from heaven and consume them, just as Elijah did?" But He turned and rebuked them, and said, "You do not know what

manner of spirit you are of. For the Son of Man did not come to destroy men's lives but to save them."

Matthew 20:20-24: Then the mother of Zebedee's sons came to Him with her sons, kneeling down and asking something from Him. And He said to her, "What do you wish?" She said to Him, "Grant that these two sons of mine may sit, one on Your right hand and the other on the left, in Your kingdom." But Jesus answered and said, "You do not know what you ask. Are you able to drink the cup that I am about to drink, and be baptized with the baptism that I am baptized with?" They said to Him, "We are able." So He said to them, "You will indeed drink My cup, and be baptized with the baptism that I am baptized with; but to sit on My right hand and on My left is not Mine to give, but *it is for those* for whom it is prepared by My Father." And when the ten heard *it,* they were greatly displeased with the two brothers.

As you can see, there is a stark contrast to how John acted early in his walk with Jesus, versus what he instructs in his epistles. His time with Jesus and the experiences of his Christian life caused the attitude of haughtiness and pride to be replaced with an attitude that reflects the Father's nature. John's example proves that pride and prejudice can be broken and replaced with acceptance and compassion. Judgment can be replaced by love.

One of my favorite examples of someone who underwent a dramatic change is James, the half brother of Jesus. Can you imagine how weird it would have been to be raised in the same home as the Son of God? Someone who had never sinned?

Never had an unhealthy thought? Said in the temple, as a child, that He was about His Father's business? The truth of the matter is that James probably didn't believe that Jesus was the Messiah, the Son of God, until later in his life.

> **John 7:3-5:** His brothers therefore said to Him, "Depart from here and go into Judea, that Your disciples also may see the works that You are doing. For no one does anything in secret while he himself seeks to be known openly. If You do these things, show Yourself to the world." For even His brothers did not believe in Him.

But James wrote one of the most instructional books of the Bible. He is also identified in several scriptures as the leader of the early church in Jerusalem.

> **Acts 12:17:** But motioning to them with his hand to keep silent, he declared to them how the Lord had brought him out of the prison. And he said, "Go, tell these things to James and to the brethren." And he departed and went to another place.

> **Acts 15:13-21:** And after they had become silent, James answered, saying, "Men *and* brethren, listen to me: Simon has declared how God at the first visited the Gentiles to take out of them a people for His name. And with this the words of the prophets agree, just as it is written: *'After this I will return and will rebuild the tabernacle of David, which has fallen down; I will rebuild its ruins, and I will set it up; so that the rest of mankind may seek the Lord, even all the Gentiles who are called by My name, says the Lord who does all*

these things.' "Known to God from eternity are all His works. Therefore I judge that we should not trouble those from among the Gentiles who are turning to God, but that we write to them to abstain from things polluted by idols, from sexual immorality, from things strangled, and from blood. For Moses has had through-out many generations those who preach him in every city, being read in the synagogues every Sabbath."

Acts 21:18: On the following day Paul went in with us to James, and all the elders were present.

Galatians 1:19: But I saw none of the other apostles except James, the Lord's brother.

That there was a dramatic change in James is undeniable. What happened to cause this change? I believe it is the same thing that gives all of us the power to turn from being domi-nated by our old habits, characteristics – even our flesh. It is the life-living part of the gospel. It is what separates Christianity from all other religions. *The event that transformed James was the resurrection of Jesus.* James was confronted with this awesome truth face-to-face!

1 Corinthians 15:4-7: And that He was buried, and that He rose again the third day according to the Scriptures, and that He was seen by Cephas, then by the twelve. After that He was seen by over five hundred brethren at once, of whom the greater part remain to the present, but some have fallen asleep. After that He was seen by James, then by all the apostles.

This passage tells us that Jesus made it a point to show Himself to James. When He appeared to the twelve and then the five hundred, they were all believers, so James wouldn't have been among them. According to this, James is possibly the only non-believer that saw Jesus after the resurrection. He had a purpose for confronting James with the resurrection. Stirring, isn't it? This had an impact on James and it appears that James' brothers also were converted. Look at Acts 1:14. It is an entirely new description of Jesus' brothers. Remember that earlier His brothers didn't believe in Him. Now look at them.

Acts 1:14: These all continued with one accord in prayer and supplication, with the women and Mary the mother of Jesus, and with His brothers.

My final example of a dramatic change is one that took place instantly. In Acts, chapter 9, Saul of Tarsus was on his way to Damascus to capture Christians and bring them back to Jerusalem for punishment.

Acts 9:3-6: As he journeyed he came near Damascus, and suddenly a light shone around him from heaven. Then he fell to the ground, and heard a voice saying to him, "Saul, Saul, why are you persecuting Me?" And he said, "Who are You, Lord?" Then the Lord said, "I am Jesus, whom you are persecuting. It *is* hard for you to kick against the goads." So he, trembling and astonished, said, "Lord, what do You want me to do?" Then the Lord *said* to him, "Arise and go into the city, and you will be told what you must do."

The change in Saul was immediate and permanent. One minute he was upright, in control, confident. The next minute he was on the ground. The amazing thing about Saul is that he immediately submitted to Jesus, and asked, "What do You want me to do?" *And that's the key that sparks real, life-altering change in every man.*

The two questions that every man must ask himself are so simple. The answers to these questions, if answered correctly, unleash the power to a more fulfilling life. This can be the end of frustration and boredom. It can begin a new era of leadership and opportunity. Saul had to ask himself both of these questions.

AM I WILLING TO LAY DOWN MY WILL AND SUBMIT TO GOD'S PLAN FOR MY LIFE?

LORD, WHAT DO YOU WANT ME TO DO?

When I mentor men regarding making changes in their lives, they tend to get nervous about it. They wonder if they can really change. Some have tried before, but then gave up after a while. I tell them a story on myself to help them relax. When I accepted a management position with one company, I often spoke at conventions, seminars and training sessions around the country. I had never done this before, and I had a lot to learn. Each time I spoke I learned some things that I could incorporate into future sessions, and eventually I became an effective presenter and trainer. But one day early in this process I was getting ready to speak to a group of students in Houston, Texas. I decided to use the restroom before the session began, and just as I was entering the restroom the

Dean of the school walked by and asked me if I was nervous. I said boldly, "Not at all. Why do you ask?" He said, "Because you're walking into the ladies' restroom!" That day I learned how to shut all of the distractions out and focus on my purpose! I knew I had to change how I prepared and how I channeled my nerves. I had to become confident in who I was and what I was doing.

I made the necessary changes and had an enjoyable and rewarding career. You can change, too. Commit to it and don't give up. Encourage yourself. Reward yourself for your success-ful steps. Remember to see yourself as God sees you.

WORKSHEET

What about me frustrates me the most? _____
_____
_____

What would I do about that if I could? _____
_____
_____

What have I tried unsuccessfully to change about me? _____
_____
_____

What are some things that I know I should change but have simply come to accept? _____
_____
_____

What are two scriptures that suggest that I don't have to carry around those old habits or behaviors any longer? _____
_____
_____

Go to momentumthelife.com/1 for a short video review of this chapter.

Chapter Two

Building a Foundation

Let's begin this chapter with a little exercise; sort of mental calisthenics to loosen up our thinking muscles. See if you can answer the following questions. You may just think of your answers, or you can write them on a piece of paper.

1. What is your favorite movie? What is the most memorable line from that movie? How old is that movie?

2. What is your favorite song? How much of that song can you sing? (Not necessarily in tune!) How old is that song?

Isn't the brain an amazing thing? I first saw my favorite movie over forty years ago, and I can still tell you many of the lines from it! Though I have only seen it a half a dozen times since then, I can tell you the names of all of the characters and can even narrate most of the movie. I can also sing along word-for-word with songs that I haven't heard for years. Some of those songs even bring crystal-clear memories with them. When I was a teenager, I played bass guitar in a rock band. Incredibly, today I can pick up a bass and play most of the songs we played four decades ago.

Now I have two more questions for you. These may prove to be a little more difficult than the last two.

1. What is your favorite scripture...with chapter and verse? ("Jesus wept" doesn't count!)

2. What scripture other than your favorite has impacted you the most in the past two weeks?

Not as easy, are they? It is amazing that so many of the Christians that participate in this exercise can list numerous movies, lines from movies and remember entire songs that they may not have seen or heard in decades, yet can't remember a single scripture in its entirety! Don't feel alone if you had difficulty with this. This chapter will encourage you and inspire you to break through that barrier. Why do you think so many Christians can so easily remember the unimportant things from long ago but have to work incredibly hard to remember God's Word? In Mark, chapter 4, Jesus gives us insight to this problem.

Mark 4:14-20: The sower sows the word. And these are the ones by the wayside where the word is sown. When they hear, Satan comes immediately and takes away the word that was sown in their hearts. These likewise are the ones sown on stony ground who, when they hear the word, immediately receive it with gladness; and they have no root in themselves, and so endure only for a time. Afterward, when tribulation or persecution arises for the word's sake, immediately they stumble. Now these are the ones sown among thorns; they are the ones who hear the word, and the cares of this world, the deceitfulness of riches, and the desires for other things entering in choke the word, and it becomes unfruitful. But these are the ones sown on good ground, those who hear the word, accept it, and bear fruit: some thirtyfold, some sixty, and some a hundred.

Verse 14 is the key. The sower sows the WORD! These verses tell us that there are three things that are designed to steal the Word that we have received from the sower. First, Satan comes *immediately* and takes away the Word. Why? Because the Word is life to those that find (take hold, grasp, capture) it and health to all their flesh (Proverbs 4:22). He doesn't want you to make the Word part of your life. He knows that if you are successful and retain God's Word, you will become a true overcomer. And even more threatening to Satan is that you will then *share* that Word with someone else and then they will be free from his power! God's Word is so important to you that the enemy comes *immediately* to carry it away from you.

Second, verse 17 tells us that when we don't have strong roots, tribulation and persecution for the Word's sake can cause us to stumble. Even when many young Christians receive the Word *with gladness* their inexperience can cause them to feel helpless when facing tribulation. These attacks can be from many different sources. Some may be family members. Others may be coworkers. Others may be friends. Regardless, they are painful and frustrating. And they are designed to rob you of the Word.

The third method with which the Word may be stolen from us is made up of the three *attitudes* found in verse 19, and *I believe this is the most prevalent and most effective method.*

These are the cares of the world, the deceitfulness of riches and the desire for other things. This method is so powerful because we are so easily swayed by all of the worldly influences around us. Though we are admonished to not strive to "keep up with the Joneses" we still do. And we judge ourselves by how we measure up to others. All day long we are bombarded with advertisements that tell us what we should wear, what we should drive, where we should live, how we should eat and what type of people we should aspire to be. And all of it is materialistic and seeks to draw our attention away from the truly valuable things in life. And, as Jesus tells us, those subtle, simple desires will choke the Word out of our lives if we let them!

The good news is that according to verse 20, there are those who hear the Word, accept it and bear fruit. The rest of this chapter will show you why the Word is critical to your growth and how you can be a fruit-bearer.

Through my years of serving God, and especially since I have seriously begun teaching the Word, I have identified thirteen things that Christians need in order to really live a successful, godly life. Obviously, there are lots and lots of things that we all could use, but I feel strongly that many Christians could really be powerful, fulfilled believers if these things are manifest in their lives. Here's my list:

Peace. We need leaders in our homes who are confident enough in the Lord to walk in an attitude of peace. It's difficult to submit to a leader who is freaking out about relationships and circumstances, fretting about decisions. An environment of peace fosters an environment of faith!

The ability to stop sinning against God. Wouldn't it be nice to be truly free from those repetitive sins that you still fight? Many men I have met have made commitments, taken vows, met with accountability partners and still wrestle with thoughts, attitudes and behaviors that keep them from an intimate relationship with their heavenly Father.

The sense (perception) to walk in His ways. Too many Christians have become frustrated by little or no spiritual growth, living a life created by a series of poor decisions. I am amazed by the number of men who ask for guidance in making decisions. They are consumed by the fear of making the wrong decision rather than being confident in making the correct one. I have had so many men tell me that they just don't know whether they are where God wants them to be, or are doing what God wants them to do. They really want to walk in His ways, and not their own. They understand where their own ways have gotten them!

Good, solid godly counsel/advice. Accurate, solid advice is such a valuable tool for leaders. The big question is, "Where do I find it?" Worldly, carnal advice is readily available, but it doesn't profit Kingdom living.

Strength to tell the truth...regardless of the situation. We live in a world of illusion. We are bombarded by advertisements on television and the radio that we KNOW aren't true. We find it difficult to listen to elected officials we no longer trust. We are even skeptical of much of the ministry that we are exposed to. But what about you? Can people believe that you are telling them the truth? Or are you someone who "bends" the truth for any number of reasons? People are drawn to honesty

and integrity like moths to a flame, and most men recognize that fact. But when faced with the challenge, many men fold.

How to answer those who taunt me. Few things are as frustrating to believers as feeling overmatched by people who belittle us, our doctrine, and ultimately our God! Many Christians become spiritual wallflowers because they don't feel equipped to stand their ground when confronted. They feel like they are experiencing the old saying, "Taking a knife to a gunfight." The reason David ran to defeat Goliath was that he couldn't stand the heathen belittling God's men, and especially God Himself! Granted, when you are belittled or ridiculed, it's not on the battlefield. But it would be wonderful to know how to respond in any situation.

Freedom from the things that hinder me. Most of the Christians that I'm around are not going to leave a church service and commit some sin. They are faithful to their wives, moral and ethical at work. But some of them are not fulfilled in their walk with the Lord because they carry around things that hinder them. Many of these things were part of their lives before they became Christians, and they brought them through the cross with them. It would be such a relief for them to be able to leave those behind and to develop as an unhindered believer.

A separation of the finances/ability connection. One of the greatest lies that the enemy uses against believers is telling them they don't have the financial resources to do something great for God. In the world, money dictates much of life. But that kind of thinking in the Kingdom keeps many good people from ever taking steps toward the dreams that they are sure

that God has given them. I believe we would be shocked to see the amazing things that people were called and equipped to do, yet were never accomplished because believers were waiting until they had enough money to act.

Safety, protection and health. Many true leaders are disqualified through illness. I want to follow a leader who is strong, healthy and virile. I want to know that he is able to trust God with his health, finances and relationships. It takes focus and determination to lead confident people, and that is diffi-cult if you are continually spending time "catching your healing." When you are hacking and sneezing, it's awkward to ask an unbeliever if he or she wants what you have!

How to outsmart people who are against me. Think about your life. Are you continually confronted with situations in which you need to "outsmart" an opponent? I am. In fact, I believe that if you are going to do anything great for God, you are going to have to overcome physical, mental and spiritual foes. Your natural skills aren't going to be enough. The problem is that you don't have the time to study every possi-ble scenario that could occur each day.

Freedom from the attraction of ungodly things. Our world has made phenomenal advances in technology. I feel that the greatest strides are in communication. Every home has at least one television, most have one or more computers and nearly everyone has some type of "smart" phone. Information is liter-ally at our fingertips. We can research any topic and have answers in a matter of seconds. Unfortunately, this communica-tion network places ungodly things only seconds away as well. Television has become so subtle that we find ourselves watching

things that are diametrically opposed to the life that we now live. We idolize and respect movie stars who speak out openly against Christianity and holiness. And ungodly images and text are literally only a "click" away. Because we are inundated by ungodly information, it would be liberating to be able to live without any attraction to it.

See clearly what step to take next. Many men who seek counsel are aware that the Word says that God directs their steps. Some even know that they are His sheep and only follow His voice. Yet they are terrified to take a step of faith. I have seen men who were literally paralyzed in the face of choosing which way to proceed. I think that men would accomplish much more if they could simply be confident in which way to step!

Eliminate the "I'm not smart (educated) enough" excuse. I have heard men state that they will do something for God as soon as they are well trained, formally educated or properly developed. How amazing would your life be if you got a revelation that training, education and development don't factor into your accomplishing what God has planned for you? Training is important. Education can be very helpful. Development and experience are also great traits. But the lack of any of these can't be used as an excuse to not be used. God will equip you to do the work He has called you to do, regardless of any outside factors! God continually calls us to defeat foes who look like they cannot be defeated. He uses us to speak to mountains. He provides answers to our incredible challenges. My pastor says, "If it's easy or convenient, it's probably not God!" So, what do you do to eliminate that excuse?

Here's some awesome news! You don't have to search all over the Bible to find solutions to these. They're all covered in *one chapter* in the Bible. Open your Bible to Psalm 119 and let's see what the Word says about all thirteen of these.

Peace: Psalm 119:165: *Great peace have those who love Your law* (Word), *and nothing causes them to stumble.* Pretty simple! If you develop a love of the Word, you will experience peace. Loving the Word calms chaotic situations. Loving the Word eliminates stress. And there is a bonus. Are you tired of stumbling about? This verse tells us that you can experience great peace...and nothing can cause you to stumble. Why? Because operating without peace leads to mistakes and uncertainty. Making decisions in a peaceful state leads to focus and concentration. It allows you to be led by the Holy Spirit rather than circumstances.

The ability to stop sinning against God: Psalm 119:11: *Your word I have hidden in my heart, that I might not sin against You!* Hiding the Word in your heart causes you to draw close to God. As you experience His nature, and as you grow in your understanding of the incredible work He has done for you (and in you), those sins that seemed to always have been a part of your life diminish. The more you hide the Word in your heart, the more powerless those thoughts and behaviors become, until they simply fall away. It's such a relief to realize that there is nothing between you and your God!

The sense (perception) to walk in His ways: Psalm 119:2,3: *Blessed are those who keep His testimonies* (Word), *who seek Him with the whole heart! They also do no iniquity; They walk in His ways.* If you seek Him with your whole heart and live the Word that has been sown into you, you can be confident that you are walking in His ways. No need to question whether or not you are on the right path. No more wondering if you are simply walking in your own ways. When your desire is to please Him, you can be sure that He will make His ways known to you. Should you try to take a step out of His way, He will bring a check that will adjust your course. He wants your life to be greater than you want it to be!

Good, solid godly counsel/advice: Psalm 119:23,24: *Princes also sit and speak against me, but Your servant meditates on Your statutes* (Word). *Your testimonies* (Word) *also are my delight and my counselors.* I love this scripture! It acknowledges that there will be times when those you face are very well qualified, even royally positioned. But the Word that you have meditated on will rise to the surface when you need counsel and will lead you to your breakthrough. The peaceful guidance of the Word of God trumps the most skilled and prestigious adversaries! But you can't wait until you are confronted to begin meditating on the Word! You must have ALREADY been meditating on the Word so that you are ready for any confrontation.

Strength to tell the truth...regardless of the situation: Psalm 119:28,29: *My soul melts from heaviness; strengthen me according to Your word. Remove from me the way of lying, and grant me Your law* (Word) *graciously.* These two scriptures tell us that if you are strengthened through studying the Word, God will literally remove from you the way of lying! That's great news. And if that's not good enough, look at verses 162,163: *I rejoice at Your word as one who finds great treasure. I hate and* *abhor lying, but I love Your law* (Word). Wow! When you develop a love for God's Word, you develop a hatred for lying. How does this happen? Because the Word is truth! As you fall in love with the Word, you are falling in love with the truth. You can't love both truth and lying! It seems to me to be a pretty simple choice.

How to answer those who taunt me: Psalm 119:41,42: *Let Your mercies come also to me, O Lord—Your salvation according to Your word. So shall I have an answer for him who reproaches me, for I trust in Your word.* The word "reproach" used in these verses literally means to taunt, or to belittle. How does our salvation come in this situation? It comes according to His Word! Meditating on God's Word, trusting that the Word accomplishes exactly what He sent it to accomplish, causes the Word to rise up inside of you and gives you the answer that the situation needs. I like to interpret these passages like this: *The Word that you have stored up inside will cause you to say the right thing at the right time in the right way to resolve the situation.* If you haven't stored any of God's Word inside, you will find that you are not equipped to answer these taunts. That's one of the worst feelings ever, because you love God and you want to be able to stand up for what you believe without fear and embarrassment. Get in the Word and be ready!

Freedom from things that hinder me: Psalm 119:44,45: *So shall I keep Your law* (Word) *continually, forever and ever. And I will walk at liberty, for I seek Your precepts* (Word). Walking in liberty and freedom is invaluable. How could anyone ever put a value on freedom! The truth is that if you will keep the Word, you will walk free from all hindrances. Those little issues that have been holding you back will be broken and you will soar. Stay in the Word and see that those old burrs never attach to you again. Do what you were called to do!

A separation of the finances/ability connection: Psalm 119:14: *I have rejoiced in the way of Your testimonies* (Word) *as much as in all riches.* Psalm 119:72: *The law* (Word) *of Your mouth is better to me than thousands of coins of gold and silver.* How can the writer say that the Word is worth more than all riches? Because the Word is life to those who find it and health to all their flesh (Proverbs 4:22). Try buying that! The entrance of the Word brings light. Meditating on the Word provides wisdom and understanding. You may be able to use worldly resources to buy an education and training, but you can't buy light, wisdom and understanding! Your heavenly Father owns the cattle on a thousand hills! He won't allow you to do without. The Word brings God's abundance to you without measure. And it does so without adding any sorrow! The world's riches are quantified and have a finite existence. Not the Word. Its riches are infinite and endless. Get in the Word and slip yourself under the shadow of the Almighty and watch what Abba Father does on your behalf.

Safety, protection and health: Psalm 119:92,93: *Unless Your law* (Word) *had been my delight, I would then have perished in my affliction. I will never forget Your precepts* (Word), *for by them You have given me life.* These scriptures should cause you to jump and shout! The Word saves you from perishing and actually brings life to your spirit, soul and body. As I stated in the previous section, the Word is life and health if we will simply FIND them. The Word is to be our delight.

How to outsmart people who are against me: Psalm 119:97,99: *Oh, how I love Your law (Word)! It is my meditation all the day. You, through Your commandments (Word), make me wiser than my enemies; for they are ever with me. I have more understanding than all my teachers, for Your testimonies (Word) are my meditation.* No enemies? Get real! The Word doesn't ever say that you won't have any enemies. It does say right here that you will be wiser than your enemies. That's even better! God is glorified through your life that way. Love the Word, meditate on it and outsmart all of those who choose to oppose you. Do something to advance the Kingdom of God today and don't worry about what others may say or do. Through the Word you are wiser than them!

Freedom from the attraction of ungodly things: Psalm 119:103,104: *How sweet are Your words to my taste, sweeter than honey to my mouth! Through Your precepts (Word) I get understanding; Therefore I hate every false way.* How do you gain the victory over the lure of ungodly things? Through the understanding you receive from the Word of God. Tired of being led by your flesh down the wrong paths? Meditate on the Word. Gain the understanding that only it brings! Grow to hate the wrong way.

See clearly what step to take next: Psalm 119:105: *Your word is a lamp to my feet and a light to my path.* Although this is a very short verse, it is one of the most powerful in the Bible. This is a classic example of how the Word can bring you clarity and confidence. Many people wonder why this verse says that the Word is both a lamp to our feet AND a light to our path. To many it seems redundant but it's not at all. My wife and I had good friends who had a fire pit built in the woods near a pond. We spent many wonderful evenings sitting around the fire and eating way too much "camping" food. Because the fire pit was some distance from the house, everyone had to walk down a long, narrow path cut in the woods. It was quite an obstacle. You had to carry a flashlight to ensure you didn't end up in the brush on each side of the path. My issue was this: when I shone the flashlight down on the path so I could see where to step and not trip on any rocks or tree roots, I would invariably walk face-first into damp leaves hanging low over-head. Or even worse, wet spider webs. You know what I mean! But if I shone the flashlight up high so I could see what was head-high and where I was going, I couldn't see the path down by my feet and was likely to trip on obstacles. That's why God's Word does both for us. It illuminates the path so we can see where to step safely. It also lights the way in front of us so we don't walk face-first into things we don't want to encounter. Everything we need to travel safely and on course has been provided in the Word!

Eliminate the "I'm not smart (educated) enough" excuse: Psalm 119:130: *The entrance of Your words gives light; it gives understanding to the simple.* In this verse the word "entrance" means to open or disclose something. The word "light" means direction. So, opening the Word gives us direction. The word "simple" used at the end of the verse simply means ignorant or uneducated. Regardless of your level of education, your wisdom and understanding come from the Word. You are qualified to accomplish great things!

I understand that there are lots of characteristics that you want manifested in your life, but I believe strongly that those that we just covered are critical for you to accomplish all that God has planned for you. I know you sensed the common origination of all of these qualities. They all are found in the Bible. The directions and provisions you need in life are provided in God's Word. If you will open it, read it, meditate on it and live it, YOU WILL BE BLESSED. An old saying says that "There are no guarantees in life." But your success is guaranteed as a believer and a doer of the Word.

WORKSHEET

Do you need to further develop any of the characteristics discussed in this chapter? If yes, please list them.

_____

_____

_____

Which verse(s) in the study of Psalm 119 most impacted you?

_____

_____

_____

What can you do to be better in that area? _____

_____

_____

What steps are you willing to take in order to grow in God's Word?_____

_____

_____

_____

Go to momentumthelife.com/2 for a short video review of this chapter.

Chapter Three

Integrity

We are living in the most difficult time in the history of our country to raise children. Not physically difficult, as we have more material comforts than ever. It's not really difficult for most families in America to provide an education for their kids. We have more social services than at any previous time. What we are lacking is character, or integrity! It is hard to find any movie stars, professional athletes, or elected officials that anyone should look up to. There are some, of course. But they aren't the ones that we are exposed to. There is a fascination in the media today for people who don't accept the standards that have made our nation great.

Rebellion is encouraged and emulated. Traditional family values are bent and broken. Honesty is almost a thing of the past. It seems as though strong, traditional values are interpreted as uncaring and insensitive, while immorality is seen as enlightened and inclusive. Religious worship is seen as narrow-mindedness. What is the result? This year alone, three congressmen have been forced to resign in disgrace because of immorality. Countless civic leaders have been indicted and punished. As an introduction to teaching this material to a group of students, I held up that day's newspaper and read many of the headlines. I started with the front page, and then the local section, and ended with the national news section. The students were in shock! Most had never just read the headlines, and the impact of the example was dramatic!

The result of this lack of quality leaders is that American families are struggling. The majority of marriages end in divorce. An extreme number of our children are being raised with only one parent in the home. Many of our teenagers look to over-exposed celebrities as their role models, analyzing their lives for tips on how to live. Educators are frustrated with the lack of discipline exhibited by students in hard-to-control classrooms but they get no support from administrators.

For Christians, this environment is the perfect opportunity to actually be light and salt! What an awesome time to be a Christian. What an amazing time to raise children. I've heard people say that they are afraid of what the future holds for their kids. Not me! I'm telling you, this is a great time for believers. The time is right for strong Christian men and women to excel in the workplace. I believe that employers are looking for employees with integrity, people they can trust.

When salespeople from around the country were brought to our corporate office for training, I was always designated "Keeper of the Van." That meant that I was given the responsibility of driving the company vehicle, taking all of us wherever we needed to go. It became something of a joke to some of the other sales people, and many of them called me the designated driver simply because I didn't drink. But I believe it was

God's favor displayed in the confidence that my superiors placed in me. It meant that I had more responsibility while I was there, but I didn't mind. In fact, that trust allowed me to use the vehicles for personal reasons. I was often able to visit friends and relatives and to see sights. I am confident that this was made possible because of integrity.

Our society has changed to the point where we have even changed how we speak. When I was a kid, the word "bad" really meant bad. Then the meaning of "bad" changed to good. And now "bad" means bad again! When I was young, "Up With People" was a popular slogan that meant we loved people. But now if we're "down" with something, we actually like it. It's hard to stay current. Here are a couple of job titles that have changed. Not the jobs, mind you. Just the titles!

Old title	New title
Garbage Man	Sanitation Engineer
Secretary	Executive Assistant
	Or, Customer Service Specialist

See how terms have changed. One night while watching the news on a local television network, I learned that someone who robs a store is no longer called a thief. I heard an attorney call his client (who was caught carrying a stolen television down the street) a "nontraditional shopper"! The incredible thing is, this is a great time to be part of a Christian family. In spite of all of the changes, God is still in control. I'm somewhat of a news junkie. And I haven't seen any headlines that inform us that God is no longer on His throne. He still watches over His

Word to perform it. The righteous still are not forsaken, nor their seed begging bread. His promises are still "Yes" and "Amen"!

Let me ask you a few questions. You answer honestly.

1. *Would you want to be judged by God right now? Right this second? Is it important to you to be judged fairly?*

2. *Could you use some guidance to help you navigate these unstable times?*

3. *If you could get it, would you like a guarantee that your children will be blessed?*

4. *Would you like to free yourself from sinning?*

5. *Would you like to be assured that you will achieve victory?*

I have yet to meet the man (or woman) who doesn't want a fair judgment, guidance and a guarantee for blessed children. I can't find a Christian who wants to keep sinning, or desires to fail in life! Understand that God wants the same for you...and has provided a simple method to gain them all: **Walk in Integrity.** Yes, that's it. I know what you are thinking. *"Let me try to think of someone in my life who is walking in integrity."* I can assure you there are people around you that are. The world is full of them. They just aren't necessarily noticed. They're not news, though they should be! And you can, too. It's not only possible. It's expected!

What is integrity? One definition defines "integrity" as character of being. In other words, *it is who you are and not what you do.* Integrity is much different than image. Not too long ago there was an advertising campaign that used the tag line,

"Image is Everything." Nothing could be further from the truth. Image is nothing. *Integrity is everything!* Your image is who people *think* you are. Your integrity is who you really are. God knows the difference. And according to the Word of God, when you choose to walk in integrity, the benefits are incredible.

Proverbs 11:2,3: *When pride comes, then comes shame; but with the humble is wisdom. The integrity of the upright will guide them, but the perversity of the unfaithful will destroy them.* How about that? This tells us that our integrity will actually guide us. So no matter how much turmoil is in the world, if you will make the commitment to be different; to walk in integrity, you will be guided through the mess and arrive where you are supposed to be! God desires to lead you from blessing to blessing. Your integrity will be your guide.

Psalm 7:8-10: *The Lord shall judge the peoples; judge me, O Lord, according to my righteousness, and according to my integrity within me. Oh, let the wickedness of the wicked come to an end, but establish the just; for the righteous God tests the hearts and minds. My defense is of God, who saves the upright in heart.* The psalmist said that he was ready to be judged...right now! How could he say that? Because of the integrity inside of him. When you are walking in integrity, God Himself becomes your defense. Wow! What else do you need?

Proverbs 20:7: *The righteous man walks in his integrity; his children are blessed after him.* Did you get that? If you will walk in integrity, your children **are** blessed! Not, might be blessed. Not, could be blessed. Not, probably will be blessed. They **are** blessed! That's as good a guarantee as you'll ever get. I understand that everything the newspapers and television say about your children's future is negative. But your children don't have to live by the predictions made by the world just like you don't have to submit to the cares of this world. You can all live by the promises of the Word! YOU live a life of integrity and the Word promises that your children ARE BLESSED.

Genesis 20:1-7: *And Abraham journeyed from there to the South, and dwelt between Kadesh and Shur, and stayed in Gerar. Now Abraham said of Sarah his wife, "She is my sister." And Abimelech king of Gerar sent and took Sarah. But God came to Abimelech in a dream by night, and said to him, "Indeed you are a dead man because of the woman whom you have taken, for she is a man's wife." But Abimelech had not come near her; and he said, "Lord, will You slay a righteous nation also? Did he not say to me, 'She is my sister'? And she, even she herself said, 'He is my brother.' In the integrity of my heart and innocence of my hands I have done this." And God said to him in a dream, "Yes, I know that you did this in the integrity of your heart. For I also withheld you from sinning against Me; therefore I did not let you touch her. Now therefore, restore the man's wife; for he is a prophet, and he will pray for you and you shall live. But if you do not restore her, know that you shall surely die, you and all who are yours."* How amazing is that story! Abraham and Sarah *lied* about their relationship by saying that they were sister and brother. So King Abimelech took Sarah, which he had a right to do. And in spite of all of that, God prevented King Abimelech from sinning against Him by keeping anything physical from happening! Why? Because King Abimelech acted in the integrity of his heart. I love this story! Integrity causes you to make good decisions, and to avoid *knowingly* entering into sin. BUT when you

are a person of integrity, God will prevent you from sinning against Him even when circumstances are hidden from you and you could have sinned *unknowingly!* That's Kingdom living.

Psalm 41:11,12: *By this I know that You are well pleased with me, because my enemy does not triumph over me. As for me, You uphold me in my integrity, and set me before Your face forever.* Walking in integrity causes your enemies to fail when they rise up against you. And God upholds you in your integrity. AND sets you face-to-face with Him forever! Are any of your enemies face-to-face with the Lord? I don't think so!

I've put together a few questions that you can use to measure your integrity. These are simply to help you identify areas that you might like to adjust, or fine-tune. They are examples of things you can use to evaluate how you are doing.

1. **How well do you treat people from whom you can gain NOTHING?** Do you treat them as though you really loved them and cared about them? In Matthew 25:37-40 Jesus said that whatever you have done to the <u>least</u> of these you have done it unto Him. Good or bad. Ouch! Better work on that one.

2. **Are you transparent to others?** Do people know the real you, or do they simply know the person you pretend to be when you are with them? A fruit of integrity is honesty and openness. This builds trust and confidence in those around you.

3. **Are you the same person no matter who you are with?** One of the greatest face-to-face confrontations recorded in the New Testament was between Peter and

Paul in Galatians 2:11-21. Peter would act differently depending upon who was around. Paul confronted him and called him a hypocrite right in front of everyone!

4. **Do you admit wrongdoing without being caught?** Have you noticed that public figures and celebrities never apologize unless they are caught? And then they seem to apologize for having been discovered. It's like they blame the exposure and not their own actions! Personal responsibility is such a rare commodity today. Men with integrity, however, "come clean" when convicted by the Holy Spirit whether or not the sin is exposed. They genuinely repent before God and even other people, if necessary. Men of integrity will do whatever is necessary to keep their hearts and lives clean.

5. **Do you put others ahead of yourself?** I think the Church of God would be a lot more relevant if Christians would begin to serve their communities. And I believe that the Church of God would be much stronger if Christians would serve more in their local churches. Jesus told us that we are to be like Him. And He said that He came to serve…not to be served.

6. **When you have an issue with someone, do you talk TO them or ABOUT them?** It hurts when you find out that people have been talking negatively about you. And doesn't it hurt even more when Christian brothers or sisters are talking about you? Don't be a party to that behavior. It shows a lack of integrity! It also shows a lack of understanding. You are never better positioned in any way when you gossip about someone else's faults.

Choose today to be different. Choose to be a man of integrity. You may not stand out among worldly men, but you **will stand out to God!** Everyone around you will be better for it. Especially your family.

WORKSHEET

Write what integrity means to you. _____

_____

_____

List a few characteristics that you admire in one or two specific men or women that you feel walk in integrity.

_____

_____

_____

Write the number of two or three of the questions at the end of this chapter in which you want to be better. Briefly state what you will do differently.

( ) _____

_____

_____

( ) _____

_____

_____

Go to momentumthelife.com/3 for a short video review of this chapter.

Chapter Four

Fire!

Have you noticed the New Testament gospels and epistles contain terms like overcome, resist, fight, stand, conqueror (or more than a conqueror!), victory, cast down, battle, war and warfare? These are just a sampling of the combative terms used over and over again. One of the most sure ways to lose momentum in your life is to allow yourself to believe you aren't strong enough to endure whatever it is you're going through. When we become weak, we begin to doubt, lose our resolve and surrender. It's pretty obvious why these aggressive terms are used so frequently in God's Word, but before we explore the reasons, I want to share a story from the Old Testament that bothered me for a long time.

The story is about Shadrach, Meshach and Abed-Nego, three men who refused to disobey what they knew God expected of them. It's an amazing story, but there is one part of the story that I didn't understand for years. Let's read Daniel, chapter 3, and then study it more closely.

Daniel 3: *Nebuchadnezzar the king made an image of gold, whose height was sixty cubits and its width six cubits. He set it up in the plain of Dura, in the province of Babylon. And King Nebuchadnezzar sent word to gather together the satraps, the administrators, the governors, the counselors, the treasurers, the judges, the magistrates, and all the officials of the provinces, to come to the dedication of the image which King Nebuchadnezzar had set up. So the satraps, the administrators, the governors, the counselors, the treasurers, the judges, the magistrates, and all the officials of the provinces gathered together for the dedication of the image that King Nebuchadnezzar had set up; and they stood before the image that Nebuchadnezzar had set up.*

Then a herald cried aloud: "To you it is commanded, O peoples, nations, and languages, that at the time you hear the sound of the horn, flute, harp, lyre, and psaltery, in symphony with all kinds of music, you shall fall down and worship the gold image that King Nebuchadnezzar has set up; and whoever does not fall down and worship shall be cast immediately into the midst of a burning fiery furnace." So at that time, when all the people heard the sound of the horn, flute, harp, and lyre, in symphony with all kinds of music, all the people, nations, and languages fell down and worshiped the gold image which King Nebuchadnezzar had set up.

Therefore at that time certain Chaldeans came forward and accused the Jews. They spoke and said to King Nebuchadnezzar, "O king, live forever! You, O king, have made a decree that everyone who hears the sound of the horn, flute, harp, lyre, and psaltery, in symphony with all kinds of music, shall fall down and worship the gold image; and whoever does not fall down and worship shall be cast into the midst of a burning fiery furnace. There are certain Jews whom you have set over the affairs of the province of Babylon: Shadrach, Meshach, and Abed-Nego; these men, O king, have not paid due regard to you. They do not serve your gods or worship the gold image which you have set up."

Then Nebuchadnezzar, in rage and fury, gave the command to bring Shadrach, Meshach, and Abed-Nego. So they brought these men before the king. Nebuchadnezzar spoke, saying to them, "Is it true, Shadrach, Meshach, and Abed-Nego, that you do not serve my gods or worship the gold image which I have set up? Now if you are ready at the time you hear the sound of the horn, flute, harp, lyre, and psaltery, in symphony with all kinds of music, and you fall down and worship the image which I have made, good! But if you do not worship, you shall be cast immediately into the midst of a burning fiery furnace. And who is the god who will deliver you from my hands?"

Shadrach, Meshach, and Abed-Nego answered and said to the king, "O Nebuchadnezzar, we have no need to answer you in this matter. If that is the case, our God whom we serve is able to deliver us from the burning fiery furnace, and He will deliver us from your hand, O king. But if not, let it be known to you, O king, that we do not serve your gods, nor will we worship the gold image which you have set up."

Then Nebuchadnezzar was full of fury, and the expression on his face changed toward Shadrach, Meshach, and Abed-Nego. He spoke and commanded that they heat the furnace seven times more than it was usually heated. And he commanded certain mighty men of valor who were in his army to bind Shadrach, Meshach, and Abed-Nego, and cast them into the burning fiery furnace. Then these men were bound in their coats, their trousers, their turbans, and their other garments, and were cast into the midst of the burning fiery furnace. Therefore, because the king's command was urgent, and the furnace exceedingly hot, the flame of the fire killed those men who took up Shadrach, Meshach, and Abed-Nego. And these three men, Shadrach, Meshach, and Abed-Nego, fell down bound into the midst of the burning fiery furnace.

Then King Nebuchadnezzar was astonished; and he rose in haste and spoke, saying to his counselors, "Did we not cast three men bound into the midst of the fire?" They answered and said to the king, "True, O king." "Look!" he answered, "I see four men loose, walking in the midst of the fire; and they are not hurt, and the form of the fourth is like the Son of God." Then

Nebuchadnezzar went near the mouth of the burning fiery furnace and spoke, saying, "Shadrach, Meshach, and Abed-Nego, servants of the Most High God, come out, and come here." Then Shadrach, Meshach, and Abed-Nego came from the midst of the fire. And the satraps, administrators, governors, and the king's counselors gathered together, and they saw these men on whose bodies the fire had no power; the hair of their head was not singed nor were their garments affected, and the smell of fire was not on them.

Nebuchadnezzar spoke, saying, "Blessed be the God of Shadrach, Meshach, and Abed-Nego, who sent His Angel and delivered His servants who trusted in Him, and they have frustrated the king's word, and yielded their bodies, that they should not serve nor worship any god except their own God! Therefore I make a decree that any people, nation, or language which speaks anything amiss against the God of Shadrach, Meshach, and Abed-Nego shall be cut in pieces, and their houses shall be made an ash heap; because there is no other God who can deliver like this." Then the king promoted Shadrach, Meshach, and Abed-Nego in the province of Babylon.

These three guys are Old Testament studs! They clearly understood the decree of the king. They knew that putting God first and refusing to bow down to the idol that Nebuchadnezzar had made would defy that decree. Yet they remained faithful. And God delivered them.

I want to show you the part that used to bother me. It is found in the answer that Shadrach, Meshach and Abed-Nego gave to the king in verses 17 and 18: *"If that is the case, our God whom we serve is able to deliver us from the burning fiery furnace, and He will deliver us from your hand, O king. But if not, let it be known to you, O king, that we do not serve your gods, nor will we worship the gold image which you have set up."*

It is incredible that they understood God would deliver them from the fiery furnace. They didn't waver or doubt. AND THEY WEREN'T EVEN UNDER THE NEW AND BETTER COVENANT IN WHICH WE LIVE! If only we would have that same resolve! But verse 18 was my problem. I couldn't understand why they added the *"But if not"* part. On one hand they said God would deliver them and on the other hand they said, *"But if not."* Why would they say that? I have a revelation on that now and I love that they added that!

I believe this was actually a statement of faith that God would deliver them. They knew He would act on their behalf. But they showed Nebuchadnezzar their love and commitment to God by telling the king that even if God wouldn't save them, they were still going to be obedient to Him. In their minds the act of bowing and worshipping another god was so foreign they weren't going to bow NO MATTER WHAT ELSE HAPPENED. They were telling the king they loved God so much that even if He didn't move in this instance, they were going to remain faithful to Him! It is similar to me saying to someone, "I know God will deliver me from this particular situation. It's a promise in His Word for me. I trust Him. But I love

Him so much that even if He didn't come through for me in this instance, I would still love Him and serve Him." The statement that I once viewed as showing a lack of faith and confidence in God is really an incredible statement of faithfulness! They weren't doubting God. They were making a declaration of their loyalty.

Now that we know where Shadrach, Meshach and Abed-Nego stood regarding God's delivering power, let's look at another facet of this story. These three men KNEW God would deliver them from the fire. And He did! But not at the time or the place where they were expecting. (And not in the manner in which we all want His deliverance.) What do I mean? Here's the stand of faith that most of us take. We say, "I'm a child of God and He loves me. God will deliver me from every fire." And then, off in the distance we see a fire. And every inch closer to the fire we get, thoughts of doubt begin to enter our minds! As we see the fire a little more clearly, we begin to waver a little in our stand of faith. And for many Christians, simply the sight of the fire causes them to lose heart and quit. Many are shocked that there is a fire in the distance! They say, "I thought God was making my life perfect. I'm a new creation in Christ...I didn't know I would actually face a fire sometime. What am I doing wrong?" And sometimes they give up at this very point.

Other Christians continue to trust God, and fight off the negative thoughts. But as they get close enough to the fire to smell smoke they begin to doubt. To be close enough to the fire to smell it causes some to give up. Many others stay strong. But when some of them are close enough to the fire to actually feel the heat, they begin to wonder if they will be okay after all. Many lose heart because of the heat. Keep in mind that NONE of the people I have mentioned so far are ACTUALLY IN THE FIRE! But just the thought, sight, smell or heat of the fire causes them to faint. Remember that Shadrach, Meshach and Abed-Nego didn't decide to bow to the idol at the mouth of the furnace! They didn't wonder where God was and why He hadn't delivered them yet. They didn't bow at all!

The reason that this story is so powerful is that God *did not deliver the three men from having to face the fire. He delivered them from the midst of the fire!* This is such an encouragement for all of us! As we take ground for God's Kingdom, and as we grow in the Word, we will face challenges, great and small. But God is faithful and He will deliver us! If we are going to be strong Christians, doers and not just hearers of the Word, we can't let the sight of a fire, the smell of a fire or the heat of a fire cause us to lose heart and give up. We can't stand in faith up to the door of the furnace. We have to be willing to walk right in and see the deliverance of God!

The Bible doesn't promise us that once we become Christians we will never have to face challenges or obstacles. Jesus didn't say that our lives would be smooth sailing every day. In John 16:33, Jesus said, *"These things I have spoken to you, that in Me you may have peace. In the world you will have tribulation; but be of good cheer, I have overcome the world."* Wow! What a timely promise for us today. That issue you are dealing with today will not defeat you if you just don't give up! Don't deny that there is a fire and you are being challenged. That won't bring the victory. Speaking the Word (in

faith) regarding your situation is what brings the victory! Your victory has already been won. The way of escape has been established. Jesus tells us in Mark 11: 23, *"For assuredly, I say to you, whoever says to this mountain, 'Be removed and be cast into the sea,' and does not doubt in his heart, but believes that those things he says will be done, he will have whatever he says."*

When your faith is being tested, don't wonder why it is happening. Don't ask where God is. James (Jesus' half brother) gave us an awesome word regarding these challenges. James 1:2,3 says, *"My brethren, count it all joy when you fall into various trials, knowing that the testing of your faith produces patience."* Let's look at a few words in these verses. First, James says to count it all joy WHEN you fall into various tests and challenges. Notice that he didn't say "if" you face them. It's not if you will face tests and challenges...it's WHEN! And the word "fall" doesn't mean simply to fall like we normally use it. It means to fall into something that is all around us, or is surrounding us. In other words, we couldn't miss it. Trials *will* be a part of your Christian life. You will "fall" into tests and challenges. The good news is these tests of our faith produce patience. Patience means ENDURANCE and CONSISTENCY. Meditate on that for a minute or two. We don't become enduring and consistent simply by reading the Bible, going to church and praying. We develop endurance and consistency by facing tests and challenges, exercising our faith and winning.

Let's stop letting the sight, smell and temperature of fires in our paths rob us of the endurance and consistency that God desires in our lives. Family contentions, financial obligations and symptoms of sickness all carry the smell of smoke. We can't let them rob us of the momentum we have fought to gain. I met with a couple after church recently and they thanked me for standing in faith with them regarding financial problems. They had been through a long, trying time, and periodically we would pray in agreement and look at promises in the Word. Throughout that time they continued tithing, standing in faith and claiming promises over their situation. And when we talked the other evening, they were so excited. They are now prospering to the point of not just getting by. They are now cheerfully giving to many good works. But it took a strong stand of faith and perseverance. It was never easy. But now they have an amazing testimony which will bring hope to others. They didn't give up when they smelled smoke. Neither will we!

For us to have a positive impact on those around us requires strength and endurance. Believe me, we really need to have a positive impact! And people, both Christians and non-Christians, need and expect us to be consistent. Our families are counting on us. Our churches are counting on us. And ultimately, God is counting on us! Each small victory we achieve builds upon other small victories and soon we have gained momentum that carries us into and through new challenges.

WORKSHEET

List a challenge that you are dealing with RIGHT NOW that you would like to get beyond. _____

_____

_____

Instead of wondering what the causes of that are, begin to speak the Word into your situation. Write a scripture that demonstrates your ultimate victory in that current situation.

_____

_____

_____

Although we would like to avoid tests and challenges, they are necessary for us to develop into overcoming Christians. What are the two character traits James tells us are developed in our lives as we overcome tests and challenges?_____

_____

_____

List some tests or challenges you have dealt with in the past that are no longer an issue for you. _____

_____

_____

Go to momentumthelife.com/4 for a short video review of this chapter.

Chapter Five

One Father's Example

Momentum is so important in our lives. It helps build confidence and support that drives out fear and doubt and causes us to look forward to challenges rather than run from them. Being surrounded by strong, faithful people will help you gain and retain momentum. Conversely, having the wrong people in your life will rob you of the momentum that you have achieved.

There are certain things I look for when choosing friends and associates. And believe me, many people don't meet my requirements. Don't take that the wrong way, and think that I'm elusive and judgmental. I'm not at all. I am very social and accepting. But I'm very careful to place my trust in someone. If I really need to depend on someone, I want to be sure I can count on them. Ironically, the characteristics I look for don't seem to me to be unique or difficult. I think they are basic things that build solid relationships based upon trust and respect. In my opinion, if someone doesn't exhibit these characteristics, I won't put myself in a position to be hurt or let down by him. I'll be friendly, kind and empathetic, but I won't become too close to them.

I have two daughters and one son, and I have learned many things about raising children. It's amazing what our kids can teach us. It's also amazing what our kids' friends can teach us! Sometimes we're out in front and sometimes we learn a little too late. But my wife and I learned early on what to look for in the kids that our daughters and son were around. We have always believed we were responsible for our children's friendships. I'm surprised by how many parents say they can't tell their kids who they can run with, where they can go and who they will be going with. I just don't get that! God gave us the responsibility to protect our children and to teach them to be wise. We need to help our kids learn how to develop healthy relationships with trustworthy friends. They need to become good "pickers."

In this chapter I want to look at the most important characteristic to me. It is the foundation necessary for building long-lasting, solid relationships. It's what I told both of my sons-in-law was most important to me when they asked for my daughters' hands in marriage. It's what I have worked to instill in my son. Very simply put, it's FAITHFULNESS.

Faithfulness, though simple, entails many things. When I think of faithfulness I think of loyalty. I think of honesty. I think of responsibility. I think of stewardship. Most of all, I think of God. It's impossible to name all of the wonderful things that God is. The Word tells us that God is love (1 John 4:8). It also says He is our rock, our lovingkindness, our fortress, our high tower, our deliverer, our shield and our refuge (Psalm 144:1,2). And Psalm 119:90 tells us God's faithfulness endures to all generations.

And what about Jesus? Hebrews 2:17 calls Him our faithful High Priest. Hebrews 10:23 says, "...*He who promised is faithful.*" Revelation 19:11 refers to Jesus as "Faithful and True." I love that Jesus is faithful. He never changes. He's consistent. He's the same yesterday, today and forever. And I am so encouraged that we can do all things through Him. A faithful life is NOT impossible for us.

There are many examples of God's faithfulness in the Bible. I'd like to show you one example of how faithful God is. It's a clear example that so many people overlook, and it's taken from several different parts of the Bible. I've heard teachings on all of these stories individually, but I've never heard them tied together like this. When I first saw this I was very excited because it brought so much clarity to each of the stories, and confirmed to me why they are all placed in the Bible how and where they are.

As God continued to prepare the lineage for the Messiah, He called Abram (Abraham) to separate himself for a specific purpose. So Abram obeyed, and took Sarai (Sarah), his wife, and his nephew Lot and journeyed to Canaan (Genesis 12). Abraham and Sarah were childless far beyond natural child-bearing age. But God had promised Abraham he would have as many descendants as there are stars in the sky (Genesis 15:5). In fact, Abraham was one hundred years old and Sarah was ninety when God specifically told Abraham he would have a son (Genesis 17:16,17); and just as He had promised, Sarah became pregnant and gave birth to Isaac. Imagine the joy they felt. Talk about a miracle!

The idyllic story of Abraham, Sarah and Isaac takes a sudden turn in Genesis, chapter 22, when God asks Abraham to take Isaac to a mountain in Moriah and to offer him as a burnt offering. Can you imagine the sorrow Abraham must have felt? And how in the world could he tell Sarah? What would he say to her? After being childless for all of those decades and then being blessed by God with a son! And now He was asking Abraham to sacrifice his only son, the son that God promised and delivered to him.

What did Abraham do? He obeyed. I don't know what Abraham was thinking. Maybe he thought that God would change His mind at the last minute. Maybe he thought that if God could give him a son at one hundred years of age, He could surely give him another one now. One thing I do know is Abraham trusted God and would do as He requested. And after traveling for three days, Abraham saw the place for the sacrifice. He unloaded his things and instructed his men to stay there while He and Isaac went to worship God. Genesis 22:5 says, *"And Abraham said to his young men, 'Stay here with the donkey; the lad and I will go yonder and worship, and we will come back to you.' "* That is an interesting thing for Abraham to say to his men since he was going to offer Isaac as a burnt offering. He was planning to come back alone.

Let's read Genesis 22:6-14 for the rest of this story. And then we'll look at some interesting things.

Genesis 22:6–14: *So Abraham took the wood of the burnt offering and laid it on Isaac his son; and he took the fire in his hand, and a knife, and the two of them went together. But Isaac spoke to Abraham his father* *and said, "My father!" And he said, "Here I am, my son." Then he said, "Look, the fire and the wood, but where is the lamb for a burnt offering?" And Abraham said, "My son, God will provide for Himself the lamb for a burnt offering." So the two of them went together. Then they came to the place of which God had told him. And Abraham built an altar there and placed the wood in order; and he bound Isaac his son and laid him on the altar, upon the wood. And Abraham stretched out his hand and took the knife to slay his son.*

But the Angel of the Lord called to him from heaven and said, "Abraham, Abraham!" So he said, "Here I am." And He said, "Do not lay your hand on the lad, or do anything to him; for now I know that you fear God, since you have not withheld your son, your only son, from Me." Then Abraham lifted his eyes and looked, and there behind him was a ram caught in a thicket by its horns. So Abraham went and took the ram, and offered it up for a burnt offering instead of his son. And Abraham called the name of the place, The-Lord-Will-Provide; as it is said to this day, "In the Mount of the Lord it shall be provided."

Verse 6 tells us that Abraham and Isaac carried the items necessary for the sacrifice and in verse 7 Isaac asked a very good question. He said to his dad, *"Look, the fire and the wood, but where is the lamb for a burnt offering?"* He saw that they had everything for the offering but the offering itself! And Abraham answered him in verse 8. *"My son, God will provide for Himself the lamb for a burnt offering."* This verse is the key to this whole chapter. We will come back here in a minute. The story goes on to tell us that just as Abraham was ready to slay Isaac, the Angel of the Lord stopped him. He had shown he was willing to actually offer Isaac, and God was satisfied. Verse 13 tells us that Abraham looked up and saw a ram caught in a thicket. He offered the ram as a burnt offering instead of Isaac. And verse 14 says Abraham named the place, *The-Lord-Will-Provide*.

What an incredible story. But there is much more to this story than I had ever seen in the past. And it has encouraged me so much that I want to share it with you! As I mentioned earlier, verse 8 holds a key. Remember, Abraham said that God would provide for Himself the lamb for a burnt offering? Let's examine that statement. First, let's look at the word for lamb used here. It is the Hebrew word, *sey*, which means a smaller or weaker lamb. One commentary has described it as a familiar, personally raised lamb. One of a flock that you know well. *Sey* is the same Hebrew word used in Exodus, chapter 12, when God instructed the people of Israel to select a lamb for the Passover meal. It had to be a lamb they had observed long enough to be sure it was without spot or blemish. They had to be very familiar with it.

Second, Abraham said God would provide a lamb for Himself for the offering. If God was going to provide a lamb for Himself, it would actually be His lamb to begin with. Another way of stating this would be, God will provide HIS OWN LAMB for the offering. And here is the third point I want to show you. In verse 13, we are told that Abraham looked up and saw a ram caught in a thicket by its horns and he offered it as a burnt offering. The word "ram" here is completely different than the word used for lamb. The word "ram" is the Hebrew word *ayil*, which means strong or powerful. This word is used in different places in the Bible to represent different things, but it is always used to depict something very strong. It is easy to see that this ram was NOT the lamb Abraham was talking about. The ram was an appropriate offering for Abraham and Isaac to make considering their situation, but it wasn't the lamb he was referring to.

And finally, in verse 14, Abraham names the place, "The-Lord-Will-Provide." He didn't name it, "The-Lord-Has-Provided," even though he had just made an offering to the Lord. I don't believe that Abraham was naming this place based upon what the Lord had just done. Rather, I believe that he was actually prophesying about what the Lord would do at some point in the future.

Let's go to another event that took place centuries later. This story is found in John, chapter 1. John the Baptist has been preaching to and baptizing people. He is setting the stage for the appearance of the Lord.

John 1:29: *The next day John saw Jesus coming toward him, and said, "Behold! The Lamb of God who takes away the sin of the world!"*

I believe that this is the Lamb Abraham said that God would provide. This is the Lamb that would become the offering He would provide for Himself. I like to think of verse 29 as saying, "Behold! GOD'S OWN LAMB that takes away the sin of the world!" This is the only acceptable Lamb for God's offering. And He had to provide it Himself! First Peter 1:19 tells us that we are redeemed through the precious blood of Christ, as a lamb without spot or blemish. Only God's very own Lamb could be the offering for man's sin. Only His blood can redeem man.

This is why I believe that faithfulness is such an amazing characteristic of God. He fulfilled a prophecy about His Lamb given centuries earlier, when His time was right. He had established His covenant with Abraham and included all of us who believe in that promise. When God offered His Lamb, it was once and for all. Jesus appeared after several hundred years of darkness for God's people. There had been no fresh revelation from God for a long, long time. People were becoming discouraged and hopeless. And suddenly here was the Lamb of God. Suddenly there was hope. Amazing!

Some historians say that the mountain where Abraham took Isaac is actually the same mountain where God offered His own Son. I don't know if that is true. But if it is, God and Abraham both took their only begotten sons, had them carry the wood for the sacrifice on their own backs, and led them up the same hill. Both sons asked their fathers about the sacrifice. Isaac asked where the offering itself was. Jesus asked if there could be any other offering. Yet both were obedient. BUT only Jesus could be the offering. Isaac could not.

As further proof of God's faithfulness, let's look at one more set of scriptures, Revelation 5:1-5.

Revelation 5:1-5: *"And I saw in the right hand of Him who sat on the throne a scroll written inside and on the* *back, sealed with seven seals. Then I saw a strong angel proclaiming with a loud voice, 'Who is worthy to open the scroll and to loose its seals?' And no one in heaven or on the earth or under the earth was able to open the scroll, or to look at it. So I wept much, because no one was found worthy to open and read the scroll, or to look at it. But one of the elders said to me, 'Do not weep. Behold, the Lion of the tribe of Judah, the Root of David, has prevailed to open the scroll and to loose its seven seals.' "*

Here we see John, as he is witness to the events concerning the end of the age. He alone has been able to enter this realm, to see God on His throne and to hear the worship of angels and elders. And yet in the midst of all of that glory and majesty, when he sees that there is a book sealed with seven seals he begins to cry because no one in heaven, on earth or under the earth is worthy to open the book! But then an elder tells John not to cry, because the Lion of the tribe of Judah has loosed the seals and opened the book! And John turns excitedly to see the Lion. But what actually he sees is astonishing!

Revelation 5:6: *And I looked, and behold, in the midst of the throne and of the four living creatures, and in the midst of the elders, stood a Lamb as though it had been slain, having seven horns and seven eyes, which are the seven Spirits of God sent out into all the earth.*

Amazing! John turned to see a bold lion and instead saw the Lamb of God that had been slain. From Genesis to Revelation, God had a plan for a lamb. But not for just any lamb. For His own Lamb. God had indeed provided for

Himself a Lamb for the offering! From Genesis to Revelation, God remained faithful to His promise to Abraham! God is faithful. Always.

There is a theory that says we become like the people we are with most of the time. Our associations are so important! It is a fact that the people we spend time with influence us in many ways. I meet many young people who believe they are strong enough to maintain their character even though those around them have none. That's a big mistake. As they grow older, it becomes clear that somehow they have adopted some of the attitudes and opinions of friends and relatives. I have seen Christians develop negative, critical attitudes that they had picked up from people that they spent time around. Some have even left the churches that they once loved and have become shipwrecked.

I assure you that if you surround yourself with faithful people, you will also exhibit faithfulness. If you surround yourself with unfaithful people, you will find that your thoughts begin to change, your eyes begin to wander and your word means less and less to those who depend upon you. Proverbs 11:3 says, *"The integrity of the upright will guide them, but the perversity of the UNFAITHFUL will destroy them."* That is a strong admonition that faithfulness is very good and unfaithfulness is very bad! God calls unfaithfulness, perversity! Character brings momentum with it. And the characteristic of faithfulness is a strong indicator to yourselves and to those who need you that you carry the energy and determination to run the race to win. You will find that not only is your life incredible, but other believers will soon be following in your steps!

68

WORKSHEET

What does faithfulness mean to you? _____

_____

_____

What other examples of God's faithfulness can you find in the Bible? _____

_____

_____

How can you be more faithful in your relationships? _____

_____

_____

At work/school? _____

_____

_____

At your church? _____

_____

_____

Go to momentumthelife.com/5 for a short video review of this chapter.

Chapter Six

Adaptation

As we have already seen, change is all around us. It's impossible to avoid it. Yet I often find myself behind the learning curve and have to have someone else (usually one of my kids) teach me what I need to learn so that I can change with the times. We have already had a discussion of the changes we may need to make regarding ourselves, so this chapter is not about that. This chapter is going to help us learn what we can do to remain calm, be peaceful and continue to be successful in this ever-changing, stress-generating world. Having momentum in our lives doesn't mean that we will never have to learn new things. But the Bible has a lot to teach us regarding how to maintain our momentum through the waves and wind that surround us.

The other day I was in a nearby city and stopped at a nationally known bookstore. I had been there before but it had recently undergone a facelift, and I was really surprised at the transformation inside the store. Beginning about a third of the way back, in the center of the store were four walls with huge, bright graphics. The walls, which were about three-fourths as tall as the ceiling, created a separate space within the store. To enter it you had to walk through one of four openings. I was amazed that a store would take away what I assumed was the most valuable real estate within the store. It literally cut off the center isle that allowed you to walk straight from the front of the store to the back. Now you had to go around this new section, unless you wanted to walk through it.

I just had to find out what this was all about so I walked into the new section and immediately understood what was happening. The entire space in the section was devoted to selling their new electronic reading device. Bright graphics, perfectly positioned shelving units, and several store employees were all inviting me to investigate this new tool for reading. I couldn't believe it. I had seen the smaller displays for these devices at other stores, and I even have an electronic reading device of my own. But I couldn't believe a store that made its money selling printed books would take up this amount of prime selling space to sell devices on which people can simply download books at home and never have to visit the store again! Obviously, the people that were in positions to create, design, develop, install and maintain this strategy knew what they were doing. No one would do something like this if it wasn't ultimately going to be profitable. And they certainly wouldn't create a system that would push their customers away from the store.

I believe they had created a strategy that was designed to meet a very important need that book readers, like everyone else today have. It's the same need that causes me to download books rather than run to the bookstore. And believe

me...I have downloaded and read a lot of books on my device. And to be honest with you, I love to go to the bookstore. Vanessa, my wife, and I will go to the bookstore, grab a cup of coffee and hang out looking at all types of things. We can spend hours there. She works through her stack of magazines and books and I work through mine. I have no interest in her stack and she has no interest in mine. It's a great system! So yes, I prefer to read printed books; to turn pages and highlight important passages. Then what is so significant about my reading device that I will forego a trip to the bookstore and my preference for printed books? What need does it meet in a way that the bookstore can't?

In a word, my reading device is CONVENIENT! I don't have to take the time to drive anywhere to get reading materials. That's a huge benefit when the weather is bad! It's also easier for me to read when I'm traveling. And I can have several different books that I may be reading at the same time, easily switching from one to another. CONVENIENCE is a big deal to us today!

There are roughly 160,000 fast food restaurants in America and the number increases daily! Around 50 million Americans eat at least one meal a day at a fast food restaurant, generating 65 billion dollars annually. We do this even though on average, the food contains more fat, sugar, sodium and calories, while providing far less nutrition and vitamins than normal home-cooked meals. Children are eating fast food at an ever increasing rate, even though nutritional information is more readily available than ever.

I have to confess, I love the taste of most fast food. But that wasn't always the case. When I was growing up in a small town, there weren't any fast food restaurants. But one opened when I was in my early teens. I clearly remember my dad taking me with him to go try it out. Boy, did he complain about the taste! He was used to the big hamburgers he grilled for us. He was used to having fresh tomatoes, lettuce, pickles, etc. The truth is, I kind of liked the meal, but I didn't tell him that. These new sandwiches, though not bad, really couldn't hold a candle to what we had at home. And they still can't. But all of us in my family eat more of it than we should. Why? Because it's convenient. Especially drive-through restaurants.

Most of us don't sit in our cars to order (and sometimes to also eat) because it will be a better meal than we could prepare at home. We do it because it's easy! That's why there is usually a line of cars. We'll do it even though the service isn't as good as we'd like. And we'll drive away and find out that one or more of the items we ordered is not in the bag! Boy, does that frustrate me. But not enough to stay away. I'll forget about it and go back again. Not convinced that we love convenience? Let me give you another example from my life.

My dad used to work for a small, family owned petroleum company. (Now, you don't see that much anymore.) I remember that he traveled often for his job, and he'd get ideas for promoting their local service stations. If you are under thirty, you probably don't even know what a service station is. At that time there were gas wars all over America, with companies offering gifts if you got your gas at one of their stations, or had your car serviced in one of the bays. I remember riding with my dad late at night as we drove from station to station checking their prices. Then we would return to "our" station and adjust

the prices to be competitive. There were inflatable balls and lots of other toys. Once there were even fruit baskets if you filled your tank! And gas was cheap back then.

My dad was really beside himself when he returned from one trip. We were all getting ready to eat dinner (at home) and he said, "You're not going to believe what they have asked us to do! They are asking us to begin selling milk and bread at our stations! Can you believe that?" As they say, the rest is history. Way back then, someone realized it might be convenient for mom or dad to pick up some milk or bread while getting gas on the way home. Talk about an idea that caught on! Now there are virtually no "service stations" any longer. Now we have quick-markets resembling small grocery stores with gas pumps out front. We get our gas, our morning coffee, something to eat, our newspapers, magazines, lottery tickets, batteries and whatever else we need to take with us. Why did that happen? That concept was developed strictly for our convenience.

Why is convenience so important to us today? It's not because we're lazy. It's exactly the opposite! We are so busy we have to find ways to save time and energy. And we have a craving for information. We strive for connection. We have become a society of multitasking. When we are at home we watch television, work on our computers and text our friends all at the same time. Texting has become one of the primary causes of traffic accidents. And we are becoming addicted to technology. Twitter went down for a while and people literally got sick! People were so dependent on the technology they had withdrawals when it wasn't available. Communication has become convenient! The other evening we went to dinner and at a table near us were four teenage girls. Their food had been served and growing cold, but none of them were eating. They were all talking. BUT not to each another. They were all on their cell phones, talking to other people. This went on for what I thought was a long time. There was very little communication at their table the entire time they were there.

Here are some statistics I found (on the internet, by the way) that show just how much time the average person spends on cell phones and watching television. You can look up information on usage of these things as well. It's pretty eye-opening! I'm using these statistics as examples of what researchers are learning about how technologically dependent we have become. I spoke to our church staff a couple of weeks ago and asked them to bring their cell phones with them. I asked them to count how many text messages they sent and received yesterday. How many the day before that? I also asked them to count how many calls they made and received (and missed) yesterday and the day before. They were surprised to find out exactly how often they used their phones. And that didn't even include sending and receiving emails. Many of the phone calls, texts and emails are necessary. We use them for work and to coordinate family rides and events. We beg our kids to let us know where they are and what they are doing. But a lot of these are simply mundane transferals of nonurgent information that could easily wait until we are face-to-face.

* Text messaging users send or receive an average of 41.5 messages per day. The median user sends and receives 10 per day.

* Those aged 18-29 years send and receive an average of 87.7 text messages on a normal day. The median user sends and receives 40 a day. (That's 1,200 per month!)

* The 18 to 24 age group sent and received an average of 109.5 text messages a day – or 3,200 per month!

* The average person makes or receives 8 mobile phone calls a day; 250 calls per month; 3,000 calls per year.

* The average American over the age of two spends more than 34 hours a week watching television. PLUS another 6 hours watching recorded programs. Removing those viewers who watch television all day or all night, the average is 4 hours a day, or 28 hours per week.

So, how do we accomplish what God wants us to do in the midst of all of the distractions and chaos? How can we possibly keep God's purpose for our lives in focus when everything around us cries out for our attention? Luke gives us a great illustration that can show us what to do. Let's look at Luke 8:41–56 and study several people and the distractions they faced.

Luke 8:41-56: *And behold, there came a man named Jairus, and he was a ruler of the synagogue. And he fell down at Jesus' feet and begged Him to come to his house, for he had an only daughter about twelve years of age, and she was dying. But as He went, the multitudes thronged Him. Now a woman, having a flow of blood for twelve years, who had spent all her livelihood on physicians and could not be healed by any, came*

from behind and touched the border of His garment. And immediately her flow of blood stopped.

And Jesus said, "Who touched Me?" When all denied it, Peter and those with him said, "Master, the multitudes throng and press You, and You say, 'Who touched Me?'" But Jesus said, "Somebody touched Me, for I perceived power going out from Me." Now when the woman saw that she was not hidden, she came trembling; and falling down before Him, she declared to Him in the presence of all the people the reason she had touched Him and how she was healed immediately. And He said to her, "Daughter, be of good cheer; your faith has made you well. Go in peace."

While He was still speaking, someone came from the ruler of the synagogue's house, saying to him, "Your daughter is dead. Do not trouble the Teacher." But when Jesus heard it, He answered him, saying, "Do not be afraid; only believe, and she will be made well." When He came into the house, He permitted no one to go in except Peter, James, and John, and the father and mother of the girl. Now all wept and mourned for her; but He said, "Do not weep; she is not dead, but sleeping." And they ridiculed Him, knowing that she was dead. But He put them all outside, took her by the hand and called, saying, "Little girl, arise." Then her spirit returned, and she arose immediately. And He commanded that she be given something to eat. And her parents were astonished, but He charged them to tell no one what had happened.

Wow! What a story. I love it for so many reasons. Let's break the story down and see what we can learn from it. I want to begin with the woman who was healed. Imagine what she had been dealing with and how she took advantage of a small window of opportunity. She had been suffering from a flow of blood for twelve years, had spent everything she had on physicians and was still sick. As far as we know, this disease wasn't killing her. After all, she had been carrying it for twelve years and was still well enough to find Jesus. But the sickness was ruining her quality of life. She was burdened with the physical side of the disease, the constant reminder that her life was not normal. She had to deal with the poverty she was now experiencing, having spent everything that she had on doctors. And she also had to deal with the psychological burden of having an illness that was considered unclean by her culture. She was basically an outcast. What a terrible way to have to live!

But somehow she had heard of Jesus, and she believed if she could just get to Him she could be healed. We don't know how she got that information. We don't know what led her to that belief. But we do know she managed to find Him and wanted very badly to be whole. I can't imagine her disappointment when she saw that Jesus was on a journey with some people, and that He was literally being thronged by a crowd. There were so many people crowded around Jesus that she had to wonder how she could possibly get an audience with Him. Not only that, she was considered unclean and had to fight through the very people who didn't want her around! Yet she managed to overcome all of the negative distractions and all of the reasons to give up on her dream, and she reached out and touched the hem of His robe. And she was healed on the

spot! And that act of faith stopped Jesus in His tracks. Verse 47 tells us that she fell down and IN FRONT OF ALL THE PEOPLE she told Him her story!

How was she able to overcome so much in order to receive the life she so desperately wanted?

* She kept her eyes on her goal.

* She refused to allow disappointing circumstances to prevent her from getting to the solution.

* She believed that her future would be different than her past.

* She fought through the horrible image that others had projected onto her.

* Her faith brought her the manifestation of her dream.

* And then after she received her miracle, she gave her testimony right there in front of all of the people who had labeled her "unclean"! She was healed when she touched His garment. His discussion with her had nothing to do with her healing. She already had it. I believe Jesus was going to let her show everyone who had scorned and excluded her how she had been healed. Think of the impact that had on those people.

Now let's look at Jairus. He was a ruler of the synagogue. He was in the least likely position to associate with Jesus! So why did he go to Jesus? He was desperate because his twelve-year-old daughter was dying. Somehow he knew Jesus was the answer. So he went to Jesus with a simple request: "Please come and heal my daughter." Jesus agreed and went with him. But as we know,

the crowd thronged Him. I imagine that the crowd was slow-moving and chaotic. And then the woman with the flow of blood stopped Jesus and He ministered to her. Jairus had to be going crazy with frustration. His daughter was dying and all of these things were keeping Jesus from getting to her. If I was Jairus I would have been pulling Jesus' sleeves and pushing everyone else away from Him. I'd be yelling, "Come on, Jesus! Let's go!"

And then the worst news possible for Jairus came to him. Someone from his house came and told him that his daughter had died. His heart had to sink. It had to be hard to breathe. But Jesus heard the news and told Jairus to keep believing and not to fear. She would be okay. And they continued on to Jairus' house, and we know how the story ended. Jairus' daughter was brought back to life! I bet Jairus needed some time to rest and refuel! What a whirlwind he just went through. His emotions must have been frayed and he had to be exhausted.

There are several things we can learn from this story as it pertains to Jairus. And we can apply them to our own lives. How was Jairus able to receive what he needed so badly?

* He left all of the traditions he had clung to for his entire life and turned to Jesus.

* He risked losing everything by going to Jesus and then letting Jesus have the run of his house.

* He told Jesus what he needed, and as always Jesus was moved.

* He had to endure the slow-moving crowd and the woman who stopped Jesus.

✳ When even worse news came to him, he trusted Jesus' words.

Finally, let's look at the story from Jesus' perspective. After all, this isn't a story of a miracle. It's a story of several miracles. Jesus was asked by a ruler of the synagogue to come to his house and heal his dying daughter. Even though Jesus hated religion and the religious leaders were seeking to kill Him, and even though the religious leaders were the subject of some of Jesus' parables and teachings, He agreed to go with him. But a crowd thronged Jesus as they were trying to get to Jairus' house. And then He felt virtue leave Him. So He stopped and had the encounter with the woman who was healed. Even with the goal in mind of healing the young girl, Jesus had time to make a connection with the woman. He then had to encourage Jairus after he learned that his daughter had died.

When they arrived at Jairus' house, Jesus saw the fear and grief, so He then had to encourage all of them that the girl would live. And even when they laughed at Him He didn't lose sight of His goal. He didn't give up and go home. He hadn't traveled there for nothing; He had a purpose. And it would be realized! He simply had them all leave and only took with Him a select few as He brought the girl back to life. I really love that then He asked them to get the girl something to eat. For a long time I wondered why He asked that. I believe that He knew that as thrilled as they all were to have her back, they might still wonder if things were really back to normal. Could she do what she had always done? Should they treat her like they always had? So He was reaffirming to them all that she was completely back to normal.

How did Jesus keep His focus and composure in the midst of all of the distractions?

* Even though the throng was great and the going was slow, He didn't send them away. He was always filled with compassion for others.

* Though His purpose for the trip was to heal Jairus' daughter, He was willing to take the time to minister to someone else. Miracles don't just happen at the destination. They also happen along the way!

* When terrible news came, He assured everyone that His purpose would be fulfilled and Jairus' daughter would be healed. He asked Jairus to remain in a place of faith. He didn't let the news keep Him from His goal.

* He didn't take the throng of people to the house. He narrowed down the distractions around Him. He hit the mute button! He eliminated the confusion.

* At the house, He removed the doubters and the mourners. The doubters spread fear and unbelief. The mourners communicated the finality of the circumstances. Jesus wanted neither around Him. Fear, doubt and bad circumstances steal our dreams and purpose.

I am confident that if we will apply the principles of these three examples, we can stay focused on what God wants us to accomplish in the midst of all of the distractions around us. We simply need to slow down, turn down the noise and walk closely with Jesus, the "Author and the Finisher of our faith."

WORKSHEET

How important is convenience to you? Why?_____

_____

_____

Describe some of the convenience items in your life that might actually create LESS time and energy. _____

_____

_____

We looked at this story from three different perspectives. Which of the three perspectives can you best relate to? Why?

_____

_____

_____

_____

As you grow in your relationship with God, and as you desire to experience a life that is different from what yours is right now, what can you change that will help you get there?

_____

_____

_____

_____

Go to momentumthelife.com/6 for a short video review of this chapter.

Chapter Seven

The War of the Wills

If truly living an exceptional life is your goal, I have a sure word for you. Some of you may be thrilled to hear it. But some of you may hate the whole concept. Are you ready? Here it is: Let go of your pride! Cast it off right now and heave it so far away you can never pick it up again. I am amazed that pride has such a strong hold on many Christians even though there are dozens (if not hundreds) of scriptures that specifically deal with pride. Can I tell you something about pride? GOD HATES IT!

I believe you will receive something from this chapter that will help you gain valuable momentum in life. And I believe if you will remember what you learn here, you will experience a freedom that you may have never known before! Our society glorifies arrogance and rewards pride. Why? Because we are lured into believing that having an air of confidence and control are essential for success. And guess what? That is true. BUT if you study Jesus' life, you will find that confidence and control, when mixed with a spirit of humility and compassion, can really change the world! But when confidence and control are mixed with pride, the result is abuse and contempt.

What is pride? I don't know what experts might say, but to me pride is simply too much self-love. Pride is self-centered and selfish. Pride is when I'm all about me! Pride leads to crime. Pride leads to racism. Pride leads to bigotry. Pride leads to prejudice. Pride leads to rebellion. No wonder God despises pride so much. God is all about unity and agreement, not selfishness. God encourages support, not isolation. And there is some incredible encouragement for all of us in the Bible about how He wants our lives to look and what we can do to ensure that His best is manifest in us.

To begin, I want you to look at 1 Peter 5:5. *"Likewise you younger people, submit yourselves to your elders. Yes, all of you be submissive to one another, and be clothed with humility, for 'God resists the proud, but gives grace to the humble.' "* I'm pretty sure that I don't want God to resist me! How about you? I read a commentary about this scripture and the word "resist" was translated **"sets Himself in battle array against."** Wow. I know I don't want God putting on His armor to go to battle against me! God must really dislike pride if He is gathering His items of war so that He can do battle against it. Many proud people are expecting God to put on His battle gear to go to war with them and to fight for them, when in reality He is putting it on to go to war AGAINST THEM!

I want to study more closely just how negative pride is to Christians. In the third chapter of 1 Timothy, Paul offers instructions on how to select bishops (overseers) in the church. Here he shows us the qualifications expected for people to be positioned as leaders in the church. These are important characteristics for those who are given the responsibility of placing

people into leadership positions. But it is equally important for those aspiring to leadership positions to understand that these characteristics are required as well.

In 1 Timothy 3:6 Paul stated possibly the most important characteristic necessary for promotion, and it is in the form of a warning! He wrote: *"Not a novice, lest being puffed up with pride he fall into the same condemnation as the devil."* What does that mean? Paul was admonishing us to be careful that we don't promote novices (inexperienced people) before they are ready. But I have seen this mistake made lots of times. It happens because we see someone who may be new to our church, and may be new in the faith. He or she is very impressive, and appears to have all of the outward qualities we are looking for. We like them and we want the best for them. We want them around...to be a part of our team. They get along with everyone and may even exhibit leadership skills. Soon we forget that they are lacking one simple but critical thing: experience. Maturity is essential for leaders. It is important for protecting the individual and it's also important for protecting everyone else. I have seen many lives wrecked because people were promoted before they were ready. The irony is that everyone involved had good intentions.

Paul tells us that someone who is placed in a leadership role prematurely may become prideful. And when this happens, he or she falls into the same condemnation as the devil. Sounds bad, doesn't it? What is this condemnation and how did the devil fall into it? I want to explore that. And then I am going to show you a stark contrast to it. Isaiah 14 tells us what pride looks like and what outcomes it brings.

Isaiah 14:12-20: *"How you are fallen from heaven, O Lucifer, son of the morning! How you are cut down to the ground, you who weakened the nations! For you have said in your heart: 'I will ascend into heaven, I will exalt my throne above the stars of God; I will also sit on the mount of the congregation on the farthest sides of the north; I will ascend above the heights of the clouds, I will be like the Most High.'*

Yet you shall be brought down to Sheol, to the lowest depths of the Pit. Those who see you will gaze at you, and consider you, saying: 'Is this the man who made the earth tremble, who shook kingdoms, who made the world as a wilderness and destroyed its cities, who did not open the house of his prisoners?' All the kings of the nations, all of them, sleep in glory, everyone in his own house; but you are cast out of your grave like an abominable branch, like the garment of those who are slain, thrust through with a sword, who go down to the stones of the pit, like a corpse trodden underfoot. You will not be joined with them in burial, because you have destroyed your land and slain your people. The brood of evildoers shall never be named."

This is what pride looks like! Pride says, "I will. I will. I will." In fact, Lucifer said five "I wills" in verses 13 and 14. Lucifer fell from heaven like lightning. That's a pretty fast and unceremonious fall! Because of his pride. His arrogance got the best of him. Here is what he was saying he would do.

1. I WILL ascend into heaven.

2. I WILL exalt my throne above the stars of God.

3. I WILL also sit on the mount of the congregation on the farthest sides of the north.

4. I WILL ascend above the heights of the clouds.

5. I WILL be like the Most High.

Pretty arrogant stuff. Especially when you understand what he was really saying. Here is what he meant by each I WILL.

1. I WILL ascend into heaven. He thought he was great enough and strong enough to make his own way into heaven.

2. I WILL exalt my throne above the stars of God. Here the word "stars" literally means principalities and authorities. He wanted to exalt himself above principalities and powers by his own strength and abilities.

3. I WILL also sit on the mount of the congregation on the farthest sides of the north. He wanted to place himself as mediator between man and God. He wanted to be the advocate for final judgment.

4. I WILL ascend above the heights of the clouds. He wanted to place himself in glory.

5. I WILL be like the Most High. He wanted to be God!

Then came Jesus, the only Son of God, filled with all of the raw power and might of heaven, yet making himself of NO

REPUTATION. His only goal was to do His Father's will. Instead of being full of pride, He walked in humility and compassion, serving everyone; those who loved Him and those who hated Him. He modeled selflessness by continually pushing the spotlight away from Himself and shining it onto the Father. Let's look at the five I WILLS of Lucifer and see who actually experienced all five of them.

I WILL numbers 1 and 2. Ephesians 1:20,21 says, *"Which He worked in Christ when He raised Him from the dead and seated Him at His right hand in the heavenly places, far above all principality and power and might and dominion, and every name that is named, not only in this age but also in that which is to come."* Jesus is seated in heavenly places far above all principalities and powers! Lucifer wanted this BUT Jesus achieved it. How? Through humility and obedience.

I WILL number 3. 1 Timothy 2:5: *"For there is one God and one Mediator between God and men, the Man Christ Jesus."* Lucifer wanted to be the mediator between God and man. BUT Jesus achieved it. Only He was qualified.

I WILL number 4. 2 Peter 1:17: *"For He received from God the Father honor and glory when such a voice came to Him from the Excellent Glory: 'This is My beloved Son, in whom I am well pleased.' "* Matthew 24:30 says that *"…they shall see the Son of man coming in the clouds of heaven with power and great glory."* Lucifer wanted to experience God's glory. BUT Jesus received it.

I WILL number 5. Philippians 2:5,6: *"Let this mind be in you which was also in Christ Jesus, who, being in the form of God, did not consider it robbery to be equal with God."* Lucifer wanted to be equal with God. BUT Jesus was God! And He brought us face-to-face with God as well!

You might also have noticed that Jesus received all of the great things Lucifer wanted. BUT Jesus didn't simply gather all of these amazing things to Himself. He has now given them all to His followers! When we accepted Jesus as our Lord and Savior, He gave all of these to us as a part of our salvation. We don't have to strive for them. They are ours. We are positioned with Jesus, and He said that everything that is His is ours as well. That means that all that Lucifer wanted...we have! No wonder Lucifer wants to wreck our lives. He doesn't want us to understand and enjoy all that Jesus won for us. He wanted it all for himself. But we have it!

If we could grasp this, our lives would be so amazing. The enemy that tries to steal, kill and destroy our lives certainly understands that we now possess all that he wanted. No wonder he is so determined to ruin our lives. That's why he works tirelessly to get us to forget who we really are and what we really have. That's why he comes IMMEDIATELY to steal the Word that we receive (Chapter Two).

Lucifer was prideful and thought he could achieve great things by his own will. But Jesus, who only sought to do the will of the Father, received the throne and all that goes with it. Through His obedience and humility, Jesus overcame every work of the evil one. What an incredible picture of what pride can do. Isaiah 14:15-21 states just how terrible the condemnation is. Lucifer didn't receive any of the things he wanted. And he is forever to be looked upon with disgust and scorn rather than awe! He doesn't even get to sleep in mausoleums or sepulchers like natural men. He can't find rest! He is an abominable branch, or sucker branch that is not connected to the tree. He is clothed with the gory and unclean garments of those who were slain. I love how Isaiah records the fall of Satan: As fast as lightning! No glory. No grandeur. No great pronouncement. Simply a fall that was so fast that a simple blink of an eye would have missed it! No wonder Paul was so adamant about not placing inexperienced and unproven people in places of leadership too soon. Please read Isaiah 14:15-21 to see what this broken adversary looks like.

To close this chapter I want to show you a major difference between God's will and Lucifer's. Lucifer was selfish and self-centered. He wanted great things, but he wanted them all for himself! All five of the I WILLs he stated were totally for his own well-being. God also has five I WILLs and they show us how He aspires to create great things. Genesis 12:1-3 tells us of Abram's introduction to God. And here we see God's five I WILLs.

> **Genesis 12:1-3:** *Now the Lord had said to Abram: "Get out of your country, from your family and from your father's house, to a land that I will show you. I will make you a great nation; I will bless you and make your name great; and you shall be a blessing. I will bless those who bless you, and I will curse him who curses you; and in you all the families of the earth shall be blessed."*

God's five I WILLs are ALL for Abram's benefit.

1. I WILL show you the land where I want you to dwell.

2. I WILL make you a great nation.

3. I WILL bless you and make you a great name.

4. I WILL bless those who bless you.

5. I WILL curse those who curse you.

Talk about having Abram's best interest in mind! Not only were these promises for the good of Abram, but they even extended to those around him. All of these I WILLs were focused outward, on what God was going to do <u>for</u> Abram. None of them were inward or self-centered.

We all have a will. How we use it is our choice. We can be prideful, focusing all of our I WILLs on ourselves. We are free to aspire for only those things that benefit us. Many believers "do their own thing" and never experience the plan that God has for them. We can strive for gain and forget that God's heart is for the white harvest that is all around us. Or we can live humbly, serve others, trust God and know that as we seek first the things of the Kingdom, He will provide everything we need.

WORKSHEET

Have you ever been associated with someone who was prideful? What caused you to come to that conclusion about them?

_____

_____

_____

Have you ever been associated with a humble person? How was he/she different than the prideful person? _____

_____

_____

In our culture humility is often interpreted as weakness. Is being humble the same thing as being weak? Why or why not?

_____

_____

_____

Jesus was the greatest leader of all time. He created a movement that changed the world. How did He keep His pride in check? _____

_____

_____

How was Jesus' obedience to the will of the Father an act of humility?_____

_____

_____

Go to momentumthelife.com/7 for a short video review of this chapter.

Chapter Eight

Help

I'm going to begin this chapter with a bold declaration. You might like it. You might think it is true. Or you might not believe it. But everything I see in God's Word confirms what I am going to say. And I can't find anything in the Bible that contradicts it. Are you ready? Here it is: GOD WANTS YOU TO BE BLESSED!

Early in our marriage, Vanessa and I were looking into buying a house, so we met with a mortgage officer where we banked to see about getting financing. It was an interesting discussion, as many young couples either have experienced or will experience at some time. In our case it felt like we were baring our very souls, and we thought that one incorrect answer would cause us to be thrown out of the office and we'd have to rent forever! At one point in the "inquiry" the officer asked us about our savings. Savings? What was that? We were so embarrassed to admit we had very little savings. But the officer said, "Don't worry about that. You're not alone. You're simply in the 'acquisition' phase of your lives." Wow, what a relief! We thought we'd been naive with our money and were really bad stewards. But we weren't. Turns out we were just "acquiring" things. Thankfully, we have since learned a lot about finances. (And yes, we really were pretty poor stewards of what God had given us.)

There is an underlying problem here, and it robs more people of their enthusiasm than just about anything else. The problem is our focus should not be on acquiring. It should be on distributing! It is so easy to develop a habit of wanting, getting and wanting more. So we get more. Then we want more. The majority of our nation is deep in debt, and ruin can come in one phone call or pink slip. Vanessa, my wife, and I, along with all of our kids and their families, live in a fantastic city. We all absolutely love it here. But we all have to guard ourselves so that we don't begin to compare our clothes, homes, cars, etc. with everyone around us. If we do that, we find that we never really measure up. Someone invariably has a more expensive car or house. Some other family has taken a more awesome vacation than ours.

The truth is, none of my family would trade lives with anyone else. We are incredibly blessed, and God's favor rests upon all of us. Yet in spite of that, in the midst of God's blessings, if we lose our focus on what the Bible says about us and what His plans are for our lives, we can easily get caught up in the momentum-robbing mind-set that we don't have enough. Vanessa and I have learned a way to defeat that greedy spirit that tries to attach itself to us. It is guaranteed to break that selfish attitude faster than anything we know of. It will bring real momentum into your lives.

GIVE! Yes, that's it. Give. Actually don't just give. GIVE GENEROUSLY! I am constantly reminded that when I was a lost, stinking sinner, God GENEROUSLY gave me His very best gift – Jesus! Not because I loved Him. In fact, the Bible says that when we hated God, He still gave His best gift. How wild is that! He's our model. He's who we should desire to be like. If He is so generous toward us, shouldn't we be as generous toward others? God wants His people to be generous. He is looking for people who will help those in need with whatever is necessary. When we do that for them, we are living examples of Jesus' love! There is a desperate world that needs assistance, and the only way they will get help is if we give it to them. It's a shame that when the subject of generosity is brought up, most people automatically think of money. Money is definitely an aspect of generosity. But generosity is about more than just money. It's about helping people no matter what they might need at any given time.

We can be generous with our money, our time, our counsel, our friendship, our prayers and our serving. Easing others' burdens is what fulfilled living is really about. Jesus was generous in His forgiveness when forgiveness was needed. He was generous with health to the sick. He took time to minister to those who needed a Word from Him. He provided restoration to those who were lost. He took time to teach the multitude in a manner that would draw them into the Kingdom. He taught those closest to Him with specific, detailed explanations of His stories so they would be prepared when He left them for Heaven. Whatever the needs, Jesus was generous with the solutions. We should do the same.

Here are a few ways we can be generous:

✳ <u>Taking time to serve others.</u> Jesus stunned His disciples when He told them in Matthew, chapter 25, beginning in verse 33: *"And He will set the sheep on His right hand, but the goats on the left. Then the King will say to those on His right hand, 'Come, you blessed of My Father, inherit the kingdom prepared for you from the foundation of the world: for I was hungry and you gave Me food; I was thirsty and you gave Me drink; I was a stranger and you took Me in; I was naked and you clothed Me; I was sick and you visited Me; I was in prison and you came to Me.' Then the righteous will answer Him, saying, 'Lord, when did we see You hungry and feed You, or thirsty and give You drink? When did we see You a stranger and take You in, or naked and clothe You? Or when did we see You sick, or in prison, and come to You?'*

And the King will answer and say to them, 'Assuredly, I say to you, inasmuch as you did it to one of the least of these My brethren, you did it to Me.' Then He will also say to those on the left hand, 'Depart from Me, you cursed, into the everlasting fire prepared for the devil and his angels: for I was hungry and you gave Me no food; I was thirsty and you gave Me no drink; I was a stranger and you did not take Me in, naked and you did not clothe Me, sick and in prison and you did not visit Me.' Then they also will answer Him, saying, 'Lord, when did we see You hungry or thirsty or a stranger or naked or sick or in prison, and did not minister to You?' Then He will answer them, saying, 'Assuredly, I say to you,

inasmuch as you did not do it to one of the least of these, you did not do it to Me.' "

It is clear from these scriptures that we are expected to be generous with our time and to help others. I am pretty sure Jesus wasn't teaching us to do these things only WHEN IT IS CONVENIENT. I'm confident that it is never really easy or convenient to offer our time like that. My pastor has said that if what you are considering doing is easy and convenient, then there's a good chance it isn't God inspired! It rarely fits into my busy schedule to receive a call that someone needs prayer in the hospital or a family needs someone to listen to personal problems. And it is NEVER convenient to visit someone in prison. But people need us. And there is great reward in it! I have never left a hospital after praying for someone that I didn't consider it an honor to be used by God.

✳ <u>Meeting material needs.</u> In the same parable, Jesus showed us that we are to help people with their real, material needs. Hungry people don't just need our prayers. They need food! Thirsty people need water. And naked people need clothes. Here's another great example. Luke 10:30-37: *Then Jesus answered and said: "A certain man went down from Jerusalem to Jericho, and fell among thieves, who stripped him of his clothing, wounded him, and departed, leaving him half dead. Now by chance a certain priest came down that road. And when he saw him, he passed by on the other side. Likewise a Levite, when he arrived at the place, came and looked, and passed by on the other side.*

But a certain Samaritan, as he journeyed, came where he was. And when he saw him, he had compassion. So he went to him and bandaged his wounds, pouring on oil and wine; and he set him on his own animal, brought him to an inn, and took care of him. On the next day, when he departed, he took out two denarii, gave them to the innkeeper, and said to him, 'Take care of him; and whatever more you spend, when I come again, I will repay you.' So which of these three do you think was neighbor to him who fell among the thieves?" And he said, "He who showed mercy on him." Then Jesus said to him, "Go and do likewise."

Jesus was explaining what it meant to love our neighbors. Then He was asked to explain who our neighbors are. In these verses Jesus explained what it means to be a neighbor to someone. Neighbors aren't only those people with whom we share property lines. We are to help everyone we can. In this story the man who was robbed had left Jerusalem for Jericho, so I assume that he was a Jew. And the hero of this story was a Samaritan. Samaritans were considered outcasts by the Jews because they defiled the Jewish religion. Jesus used this parable to show that the religious leaders didn't offer help to the man who was beaten. They were too busy. Possibly they simply didn't care. But a man who wasn't even supposed to associate with a Jewish man went out of his way to help. He was emphasizing that we are supposed to help even those with whom we don't normally mix. No prejudice allowed. No one is exempt. Those in need are our neighbors.

* <u>Generously supporting the church financially.</u> One day Jesus was watching how and what people were giving in the temple when He saw something that caught His attention. In fact, it was important enough to Him that He called His disciples to Him and He taught them about generous giving. Mark 12:41-44: *Now Jesus sat opposite the treasury and saw how the people put money into the treasury. And many who were rich put in much. Then one poor widow came and threw in two mites, which make a quadrans. So He called His disciples to Himself and said to them, "Assuredly, I say to you that this poor widow has put in more than all those who have given to the treasury; for they all put in out of their abundance, but she out of her poverty put in all that she had, her whole livelihood."*

I love how the Bible shows us not only how we are supposed to live; but it also shows us how we CAN live that way. It touched Jesus' heart when that poor widow gave all that she had. Why do you think it mattered so much to Him? What did He see in that act? Why call the disciples over and show it to them? I think the widow displayed vulnerability and trust. She gave the very best offering that she could. It wasn't nearly as much as what many of the wealthy were giving. But to Jesus she gave more than they did! It reminds me that Jesus, when nothing else would suffice, while hanging on the cross gave His forgiveness to those who crucified Him. He gave His mother a new home and family. And He gave His best gift, Himself, for all of mankind.

There are two individuals who are well-known characters in the Bible. We know one by name, but the other we only know by deed. Both men were confronted with pretty much the same scenario, and how they responded teaches us a lot about attitudes toward generosity. Matthew, chapter 19, tells us about the first man. Matthew 19:16-22: *Now behold, one came and said to Him, "Good Teacher, what good thing shall I do that I may have eternal life?" So He said to him, "Why do you call Me good? No one is good but One, that is, God. But if you want to enter into life, keep the commandments." He said to Him, "Which ones?" Jesus said, "'You shall not murder,' 'You shall not commit adultery,' 'You shall not steal,' 'You shall not bear false witness,' 'Honor your father and your mother,' and, 'You shall love your neighbor as yourself.'" The young man said to Him, "All these things I have kept from my youth. What do I still lack?" Jesus said to him, "If you want to be perfect, go, sell what you have and give to the poor, and you will have treasure in heaven; and come, follow Me." But when the young man heard that saying, he went away sorrowful, for he had great possessions."*

What a tragic story. Here was a man who was sincere in his desire to achieve Kingdom living here on earth. And as long as the requirements didn't touch his treasure, he was in. But when Jesus saw through his false sincerity, He put a higher demand on the man. He was to sell what he had, give that money to the poor and follow Jesus. And the young man couldn't do it. He wasn't generous. He was "possessed" by his possessions. He reminds me of what John 6:66 tells us. When Jesus' teaching got too contrary to what the disciples wanted to hear, many of them turned away and didn't walk with Jesus any longer. Can you imagine that? And in this instance, this young man could have simply gotten rid of his material possessions, used the money to help a lot of hurting people and then walked with Jesus and experienced a life beyond anything he could have imagined.

The second man I want to look at is Barnabas. Most of you have heard of Barnabas. You know that he traveled with the Apostle Paul (Acts 11:25; Acts 12:25) and ministered in many cities. And you probably remember that Barnabas and Paul had a disagreement that caused them to go different directions (Acts 15:36). But let's learn some other things about Barnabas. Prior to his encounter with Jesus, Saul was a very dangerous man to the early believers, and he was violent in persecuting them. When Saul (Paul) became a believer, he preached for some time outside of Jerusalem. At a point in time, his life was in danger, so he traveled to Jerusalem to join the believers there. But they were afraid of him. Acts 9:26-28: *"And when Saul had come to Jerusalem, he tried to join the disciples; but they were all afraid of him, and did not believe that he was a disciple. But Barnabas took him and brought him to the apostles. And he declared to them how he had seen the Lord on the road, and that He had spoken to him, and how he had preached boldly at Damascus in the name of Jesus. So he was with them at Jerusalem, coming in and going out."*

We see from this passage that Barnabas had enough influence that the disciples received Paul when Barnabas brought him to them. Barnabas was well-known and trusted by the disciples. Let's go to where Barnabas is first mentioned in the book of Acts. Here we will begin to understand how he had gained their trust. Acts 4:32-35: *"Now the multitude of those who believed were of one heart and one soul; neither did anyone say that any of the things he possessed was his own, but they had all things in common. And with great power the apostles gave witness to the resurrection of the Lord Jesus. And great grace was upon them all. Nor was there anyone among them who lacked; for all who were possessors of lands or houses sold them, and brought the proceeds of the things that were sold, and laid them at the apostles' feet; and they distributed to each as anyone had need."*

We can see from these verses that the early believers were very generous. They were in unity and none had any lack. And there was power in the church. Let's read on and meet Barnabas. Acts 4:36,37: *"And Joses, who was also named Barnabas by the apostles (which is translated Son of Encouragement), a Levite of the country of Cyprus, having land, sold it, and brought the money and laid it at the apostles' feet."* Barnabas was a land owner, and he sold his land and gave it to the body of believers. He was completely committed to the common purpose of helping meet others' needs.

It is easy to compare the young man and Barnabas. The rich, young man just couldn't sacrifice the material things in his life in order to meet the needs of others. He was close enough for Jesus to give him simple instructions that caused him to examine his heart, and he just couldn't follow any longer. Barnabas, on the other hand, was able to rid himself of his property and help meet the needs of others. We have forgotten the rich man as he walked away sorrowfully. But we remember Barnabas. He became an important member of the growing

body of believers in the book of Acts and a traveling companion of the Apostle Paul.

Isn't the Word encouraging? I'm certainly not recommending that everyone go out and sell all of their possessions. But we can simplify our lives by becoming less attached to material things and becoming more generous with what we have. God wants us to be materially blessed. He wants our lives to be full to overflowing. He just doesn't want us to be materially bound. Because of the simple truth found in Luke 12:34, *"For where your treasure is, there your heart will be also,"* it is important that we are generous people. It's important for us personally, and it is important to us as the church. I truly believe that generous people are close to the heart of God. Generous people can be trusted. Generous people are good leaders. Generous men make good providers. And a generous spirit will provide the momentum to live more prosperous and fulfilling lives.

God trusts generous people. He wants to bless giving people because they will be channels for His abundance to flow to others. Look at this. Second Corinthians 9:8: *"And God is able to make all grace abound toward you, that you, always having all sufficiency in all things, may have an abundance for every good work."* Wow! That's how I want to live. Don't you want to have an abundance so that you are able to give to every good work? So many people tell me, "When I get ahead financially I will give to all of the things I want to support. But I just don't have enough right now. I can't even tithe." I know they mean well, but through the years I have seen that many of those same people were unable to reach the point where they could give like had they once dreamed. "Abundance" and "more than enough" remained unattainable goals. They were never able to experience freedom from financial bondage.

The key to achieving this goal is found in the two verses leading up to verse 8. Second Corinthians 9:6,7: *"But this I say: He who sows sparingly will also reap sparingly, and he who sows bountifully will also reap bountifully. So let each one give as he purposes in his heart, not grudgingly or of necessity; for God loves a cheerful giver."* How much money is considered too little? How much money is considered bountiful? God isn't interested in an amount. He is interested in our heart! He looks at our attitude. Remember how impressed Jesus was with the poor widow who gave just two mites? It wasn't how much money she gave. It was how much of HERSELF she gave. Whether we have a little or a lot, we can give enough to make a difference. We are to start where we are and be as generous as we can be. God will bring more to us.

To see what generosity means to God, we only have to look at a few Proverbs.

Proverbs 19:17: *"He who has pity on the poor lends to the Lord, and He will pay back what he has given."* I like the *Message Translation: "Mercy to the needy is a loan to God, and God pays back those loans in full."* Pretty clear, isn't it? When we are generous to those in need with our time, our willingness to serve or with our money, God promises to repay what we have invested. And I guarantee He won't be like the unworthy steward (Matthew 25:24) who took the one talent, buried it and gave it back to the master with no interest. God repays with generosity! He only gives His best!

Proverbs 22:9: *"He who has a generous eye will be blessed, for he gives of his bread to the poor."* The *Message Translation* says, *"Generous hands are blessed hands because they give bread to the poor."* Generous eyes and hands are blessed! That's a great word.

Proverbs 11:25: *"The generous soul will be made rich, and he who waters will also be watered himself."*

Let's be generous people. Let's learn to focus outwardly and help meet the needs of others. Let's be cheerful givers and let's experience momentum in our lives every day! Do you need the wind back in your sails? Give. Give generously.

WORKSHEET

When it comes to your time and money, how would you describe yourself? _____

_____

_____

Do you know any generous people? Describe their lives.

_____

_____

_____

What could you do to be more generous?_____

_____

_____

Write a scripture or two regarding generosity. _____

_____

_____

List some "good works" that you would like to give towards at some point. _____

_____

_____

What is your plan to get there?_____

_____

_____

Go to momentumthelife.com/8 for a short video review of this chapter.

Chapter Nine

Above Everything Else

When I first began working on this book, I found myself looking more closely at my life, the lives of my family members and those of my friends. I also began to pay more attention to the lives of people at work and at church. I don't know how to determine who has momentum other than looking at actual lives and asking questions like, "Are they happy? Are their families happy? Are they prosperous? Do they have any testimonies about overcoming adversity? Are they producing good fruit?" I began to see that people need some specific things in order to obtain and maintain their "edge" in life. I'd like to ask a few simple questions.

What do you need if…

* You are financially broke?

* You are stressed out?

* You are sick?

* You are confused?

* You are beaten down?

✳ You have a rebellious attitude?

✳ You are emotionally drained?

Everybody faces different challenges, and everyone has unique needs. It's easy to see that if you are in a financial hole that you need money. If you are sick in your body, you need health. If you are confused, you need direction. But it is possible we haven't looked deeply enough. Maybe we have not asked the right questions and listened for the correct answers.

If we will simply search the Bible for revelation and ask the Holy Spirit to guide us into all truth, we will discover principles that bring light to our situations and lead us to victory over the mountains we face! Regardless of the type of mountain. I want to share a story from the life of one of the greatest men of the New Testament, the Apostle Paul. The story is found in 2 Corinthians, chapter 12, verses 6 through 10.

2 Corinthians 12:6-10: *For though I might desire to boast, I will not be a fool; for I will speak the truth. But I refrain, lest anyone should think of me above what he sees me to be or hears from me. And lest I should be exalted above measure by the abundance of the revelations, a thorn in the flesh was given to me, a messenger of Satan to buffet me, lest I be exalted above measure. Concerning this thing I pleaded with the Lord three times that it might depart from me. And He said to me, "My grace is sufficient for you, for My strength is made perfect in weakness." Therefore most gladly I will rather boast in my infirmities, that the power of Christ may rest upon me. Therefore I take pleasure in infirmities, in reproaches, in needs, in persecutions, in*

distresses, for Christ's sake. For when I am weak, then I am strong.

Paul wanted people to hear his message, but not to put him on a pedestal. He wanted to refrain from boasting, and in the few verses leading to this section he mentions a couple of men with incredible testimonies. He didn't want to be one of them. He didn't want to be perceived as bragging about his amazing life. But he did share one challenge he had experienced. And it has led to a lot of controversy and debate. What was Paul's thorn in the flesh? That's a good question.

My question isn't "What was his thorn in the flesh?" My question is, "Why didn't he actually tell us what it was?" Paul is easily one of the best-known characters in the Bible. Not only was he written about in the book of Acts, but he also wrote most of the epistles! He has given us dynamic insight into what our lives are to be like and what we need to be successful. Why would he accidentally leave this so vague?

Actually, I don't think he did. I think he was intentional in what he wrote to the Corinthians. I believe that by not telling us exactly what he was referring to, he showed us that the thorn was really unimportant! What? Paul wasn't interested in sharing what specific things he faced. He was much more concerned that we understand the victory. I love that he didn't write, "I had cancer." Or, "I was depressed." Or, "I was so poor I couldn't even get food."

Paul has actually set us all free by stating it the way he did. If he had given a name to whatever he had faced, we would all then say, "Well, that worked for _____. But Paul didn't mention my predicament so it must not be true for my situation." And countless people would give up because Paul didn't mention their issue by name. Instead, he taught us a principle that would be relevant REGARDLESS of our challenge. The thorn wasn't the point. THE VICTORY WAS THE POINT! The victory is all-inclusive. It isn't limited to specific thorns. It is available for us in every situation.

I have heard it taught that after Paul's encounter with the Lord, he just resigned to the fact that he would have this thorn for the rest of his life. I don't agree with that. That would be like saying the Lord told Paul, "Just get used to it and stop complaining!" I don't see that being part of God's character, and I don't see any indication that was the case. In fact, we see that Paul caught what the Lord was teaching him about that thorn. Let's look at several things from this story that will help us.

1. Paul said that he was boasting IN infirmities, and not ABOUT them. What's the difference? Paul didn't want to appear proud that he had challenges. He wasn't bragging about carrying these thorns around. That would simply glorify the flesh. I know people who are carrying around great burdens of all shapes and sizes as though this offers some kind of encouragement to others. Almost like a badge of courage. They say, "I'm managing okay." I don't think that managing issues using your own ability is receiving the grace of God in those areas. We'll look at this further a little later.

2. The word GRACE is important. It is from the Greek word, *charis. Charis* means gracious or gratifying; acceptable, benefit, favor, gift, liberality, pleasure.

3. Finally, let's look at a very important word in this story. It is the word SUFFICIENT. Paul noted that the Lord said that His grace was SUFFICIENT for Paul. What did that mean? Sufficient for what? The word SUFFICIENT is the Greek word *arkeo,* and it portrays the idea of raising a barrier; warding off; to avail. Its root, *airo,* literally means "to lift up or to take away; loose, put away, remove, take." I believe the truth of this story is that the Lord said to Paul, "Don't keep asking for what I have ALREADY provided. YOU are already filled with My sufficiency. YOU remove the thorn! Use My strength in your weakness! How? BY FAITH! YOU speak to it and command it to go! Put up a fight. Pray the promises in faith."

Why do I believe that? Let's look at a couple of scriptures that will shed some light upon this. Luke 2:40 says about Jesus, *"And the Child grew and became strong in spirit, filled with wisdom: and the grace of God was upon Him."* This is talking about the <u>young boy</u> Jesus. This story is about the human side of Jesus. His God side wouldn't need to grow, wax strong in spirit or be filled with wisdom. But His natural side would. His body had to grow. He had to grow stronger and wiser. It's interesting to note that the word "grace" here is the exact word that the Lord told Paul was sufficient to handle the thorn. So we see that the boy Jesus had grace upon Him.

Luke 2:52 says, *"And Jesus increased in wisdom and stature, and in favor with God and men."* Now we are looking at the <u>twelve-year-old</u> Jesus. He's growing up, getting older and stronger. And it's interesting that God inspired Luke to use the word FAVOR. What does Luke mean here? He said that grace was upon Jesus in verse 40. But here he says that Jesus was increasing in favor. Guess what? It's the same word: *CHARIS!* It can be translated grace or favor. Jesus grew in grace and favor.

My point is, aren't we children of God? Aren't we joint-heirs with Jesus, seated in heavenly places with Him, far above all principalities and powers? Isn't everything that was Jesus' now ours? The grace and favor that was upon Jesus is also upon us. So we have everything that is SUFFICIENT to be free from our thorns. We have ALL-SUFFICIENCY for every situation inside of us. Just like Paul! We really need to understand that.

I want to show you why I don't believe that Paul simply carried that thorn around for the rest of his life. And it's why I don't believe that God expects believers today to carry thorns around. That thorn in Paul's life was a plague. What is a plague? A plague is something that isn't terminal; it won't kill you. It simply ruins your life. It robs you of your joy. It distracts you from your purpose. It slows you down. It affects your attitude. It's a bummer. That's what this thorn was for Paul. So what is Paul's (and our) example for how Jesus dealt with plagues?

Mark 5:25-29 gives us the answer.

Mark 5:25-29 (King James): *"And a certain woman, which had an issue of blood twelve years, and had suffered many things of many physicians, and had spent all that she had, and was nothing bettered, but rather grew worse, when she had heard of Jesus, came in the press behind, and touched his garment. For*

she said, If I may touch but his clothes, I shall be whole. And straightway the fountain of her blood was dried up; and she felt in her body that she was healed of that plague."

The *King James Translation* tells us that the woman's illness was a PLAGUE. And what happened? She decided enough was enough! We don't know what caused her to seek Jesus, but we do know that she overcame a lot of obstacles to get there. And she went away free from the plague! And I believe that Paul did, too. What made her whole? The same thing that makes us whole today…FAITH. God's grace is sufficient to remove our thorns and to carry them away. We simply have to believe it and speak it, to act on it.

Why did I begin this chapter with those questions about needs in our lives? Which one best describes your condition today? I believe that Paul had the answer to all of the questions. Here's what I believe that Paul thought was extremely important for us. It's what he encouraged every believer to experience.

- ✳ Romans 1:1-7…Grace to you and peace from God our Father and the Lord Jesus Christ.

- ✳ 1 Corinthians 1:1-3…Grace to you, and peace from God our Father and the Lord Jesus Christ.

- ✳ 2 Corinthians 1:1-3…Grace to you, and peace from God our Father and the Lord Jesus Christ.

- ✳ Galatians 1:1-3…Grace to you, and peace from God the Father and our Lord Jesus Christ.

* Ephesians 1:1,2…Grace to you, and peace from God our Father and the Lord Jesus Christ.

* Philippians 1:1,2…Grace to you and peace from God our Father and the Lord Jesus Christ.

* Colossians 1:1-3…Grace to you and peace from God our Father and the Lord Jesus Christ.

* 1 Thessalonians 1:1…Grace to you and peace from God the Father and the Lord Jesus Christ.

* 2 Thessalonians 1:2…Grace to you and peace from God our Father and the Lord Jesus Christ.

* 1 Timothy 1:1,2…Grace, mercy, and peace from God our Father and Jesus Christ our Lord.

* 2 Timothy 1:1,2…Grace, mercy, and peace from God the Father and Christ Jesus our Lord.

Get the picture? I believe that Paul caught what Jesus had told him about grace being SUFFICIENT. So should we. Let's stop carrying unnecessary thorns. Let's stop living ordinary lives and move to a higher level. Let's apply the grace (favor) that we have been freely given. Let's experience the authority that is ours. Let's trust God and speak to the mountains and watch them go! His grace is always sufficient for us!

WORKSHEET

Define "GRACE." _____
_____
_____

Do you have any plagues in your life? Yes   No   Explain:
_____
_____
_____

How can you apply grace to that situation? _____
_____
_____

How can you help those around you break free from their plagues? _____
_____
_____

Go to momentumthelife.com/9 for a short video review of this chapter.

Conclusion

Momentum is a difficult concept to define. But it is easy to identify. You know when you have it and you know when you don't. You can feel momentum when you are watching or playing sports. Momentum can switch from one team to the other depending on specific events that occur during a game. You can feel it live at the stadium or arena. You can even sense it while watching a game on TV. The key is to gain the momentum and not to let it get away. The goal is to control as many of the circumstances as you can and make few errors. Winners overcome adversity and circumstances.

Momentum is equally important in our everyday lives. Sales people can recognize it when they have it. Sales calls become strategic and closing deals seems easy. Planning is not a chore. They wake up excited, looking forward to the day's challenges.

Political campaigns work diligently for momentum. And then they spend millions of dollars polling to try to see which candidate has it. Each side wants it going down the stretch.

We need momentum in our homes. Our marriages are stronger and more enjoyable when we have it. And when it is

missing, communication is more difficult. Agreement isn't easy. There isn't as much joy.

God wants you blessed! He wants you to enjoy abundance. He wants to watch you as you help to change the lives of others. Let's practice what we've learned from this book. If necessary read it again. Allow the scriptures to come alive in your hearts.

Let's:

* Be willing to change. We CAN be the people that God intends us to be.

* Make the Word THE priority in our lives. It is life and health to us if we will find it.

* Live with integrity. We want people to count on us. We want them to trust us.

* Run toward the fires that we encounter in our paths. Feel the heat and smell the smoke!

* Be faithful.

* Stay focused when chaos and confusion are all around us.

* Remain humble. Pride leads to destruction. But the humble are lifted up.

* Be generous. Let's help as many people as possible.

* Walk in grace (favor) and rid ourselves of our thorns.

Author Contact

To learn more about Scott and to order additional copies of *moMENtum*, please go to momentumthelife.com.

For speaking engagements, Scott may be reached at jonscotthouston@gmail.com. *What people are saying:*

"Your seminar was timely and well-presented." —K. A., Virginia.

"Four words I would use to describe your session: Informative, valuable, useful, wow!" —J. B., Texas.

"Thank you for taking time to work with us. I feel much better prepared, and I can't wait to put many of the principles you presented into practice." —P. L., Iowa.

"This is the second time I have taken this course, and it continues to be my favorite. People need this information!" —K. F., Oklahoma.

Notes

Notes

Notes

Notes

Notes

Notes

Notes